# The Emerging Research Library

The chapters included in this book were developed from papers presented at "The Emerging Research Library: Our Role in the Digital Future" Conference sponsored by the University of Oklahoma Libraries. These chapters explore the emergence of a new form of academic library and the challenging issues we face as a profession because of the changing role of the academic library. Issues discussed include the changing profession, new publishing models, the reallocation of spaces, the preservation of past knowledge, changing user behaviours, and improving access to information. This book also provides possible suggestions for helping academic libraries transition into the future, including re-evaluation of professional expectations and abandoning past practices, enhancing the use of metadata, responding to user behaviours, long-term planning for preservation, the promotion of open access initiatives, and extending professional inclusion and collaboration. Each chapter engages the question of how academic libraries will adapt to the challenges arising from their new role as facilitators of research in the information age. Together these chapters present an impressive set of reflections on the changes that are necessary for emerging research libraries to flourish in an increasingly digital future, and this book is recommended reading for scholars and professional librarians.

This book was published as a special issue of the *Journal of Library Administration*.

**Sul H. Lee** is Peggy V. Helmerich Chair and professor of Library and Information Studies at the University of Oklahoma and dean of University of Oklahoma Libraries. Professor Lee has taught in the School of Library and Information Sciences and directs a major university research library with a collection exceeding 5 million volumes. He has served as professor and dean at the University of Oklahoma since 1978 and is the senior dean on the University of Oklahoma campus in Norman, Oklahoma.

# The Emerging Research Library

Our Role in the Digital Future

Edited by Sul H. Lee

LONDON AND NEW YORK

First published 2010 by Routledge
2 Park Square, Milton Park, Abingdon, Oxon, OX14 4RN

Simultaneously published in the USA and Canada
by Routledge
270 Madison Avenue, New York, NY 10016

*Routledge is an imprint of the Taylor & Francis Group, an informa business*

© 2010 Taylor & Francis

Typeset in Times by Value Chain, India
Printed and bound in Great Britain by MPG Books Group, UK

All rights reserved. No part of this book may be reprinted or reproduced or utilised in any form or by any electronic, mechanical, or other means, now known or hereafter invented, including photocopying and recording, or in any information storage or retrieval system, without permission in writing from the publishers.

*British Library Cataloguing in Publication Data*
A catalogue record for this book is available from the British Library

ISBN10: 0-415-54323-1
ISBN13: 978-0-415-54323-1

# CONTENTS

Introduction — vii

A Tribute to Duane Webster — ix
  *Sul H. Lee*

1 Local to Global: The Emerging Research Library — 1
  *Lizabeth A. Wilson*

2 Partners in Knowledge Creation: An Expanded Role for Research Libraries in the Digital Future — 14
  *Mary M. Case*

3 Reinventing Our Work: New and Emerging Roles for Academic Librarians — 30
  *Lori A. Goetsch*

4 Attitudes and Behaviors in the Field of Economics: Anomaly or Leading Indicator — 46
  *Kevin Guthrie*
  *Ross Housewright*

5 Unintended Consequences: A Friendly User Looks at User-Friendly Digitization — 67
  *Jack A. Siggins*

6 From Advocacy to Implementation: The NIH Public Access Policy and Its Impact — 79
  *Heather Dalterio Joseph*

7 Deconstructing the Library: Reconceptualizing Collections, Spaces and Services — 90
  *Sarah M. Pritchard*

8  Out of the Gray Times: Leading Libraries into the Digital
   Future                                                    105
     *Deborah Jakubs*

   Index                                                     119

# Introduction

The papers included in this book will explore the emergence of a new form of academic library and the challenging issues we face as a profession because of the changing role of the academic library. They were originally delivered at a conference entitled "The Emerging Research Library: Our Role in the Digital Future," sponsored by the University of Oklahoma Libraries and held March 6-7, 2008 in Oklahoma City. Betsy Wilson, Dean of Libraries at the University of Washington, opened the conference discussion by challenging the traditional roles of academic librarians and questioning whether some services may no longer be relevant to our changing research community. She concluded that the profession needs to explore how collective strategic planning and subsequent decision-making might help to address research needs on a global scale.

Mary Case, University Librarian at the University of Illinois at Chicago, explores the partnerships academic libraries might undertake while retaining some of our traditional roles from the past that emphasize the philosophy of librarianship. She argues that collaborative efforts can include metadata creation and shared repositories that will help preserve and provide perpetual access to the diverse and robust collections contained in academic libraries across the nation.

Lori Goetsch, Dean of Libraries at Kansas State University, presents a framework for repurposing traditional roles of librarians while creating new positions that meet the demands of changing faculty and student demographics. While performing meta-analysis of recent job postings, she finds that these changes in the definitions of new positions benefit library users while impacting librarians in sometimes unanticipated ways.

Changing attitudes and behaviors among library users are sometimes alarming to the profession. Kevin Guthrie, President of Ithaka, focuses on economics as a specific discipline for further investigation of this phenomenon through survey and interview analysis. His findings reveal that many of the traditional services we revere do not correlate with the desires and needs of researchers who oftentimes remain unaware of the work that goes on behind the scenes at academic libraries to support online subscriptions and resources.

Jack Siggins, University Librarian at George Washington University, provides us with the wisdom that can only come from having worked so many years in academic libraries. In his paper, he addresses the benefits and consequences of the rapid pace of technology development and obsolescence. In our rush to change from our traditional roles, he identifies many possible pitfalls that may have long-term impact on our libraries.

Although work has been going on for some time to address issues of open access in scholarly communication, Heather Joseph, Executive Director for the Scholarly Publishing & Academic Resources Coalition, provides us with an overview of recent changes to federal requirements on scientific research. Recent legislation now requires all National Institutes of health funded research to be deposited in the PubMed Central repository. This significant step for open access is detailed in this paper with suggestions for facilitating communication about these requirements at the local campus level.

Sarah Pritchard, Charles Deering McCormick University Librarian at Northwestern University, takes a different approach to envisioning the roles of academic libraries in the future. Attempting to reconceptualize our libraries, she argues that a newly transformed and inclusive profession will emerge based less upon information control and more upon supporting broad access to information.

Our last paper is presented by Deborah Jakubs, Rita DiGiallonardo Holloway University Librarian and Vice Provost for Library Affairs at Duke University. Borrowing from the words of a young child comparing color television to the old days of black and white, Jakubs describes how our own perceptions of the past might influence our vision of the future roles of libraries in constrictive ways. She argues that a new view of the emerging research library requires us to abandon many of our older practices while embracing professional changes that are more consistent with current trends in the academic community.

Each of these papers engages the question of how academic libraries will adapt to the challenges arising from their new role as facilitators of research in the information age. Together they present an impressive set of reflections on the changes that are necessary for emerging research libraries to flourish in the increasingly digital future.

# A Tribute to Duane Webster

## Sul H. Lee

In everyone's professional life there are people who become mentors and models for emulation. They are the people who lead and others readily follow. All fields of endeavor have them, and librarianship is no exception. One person who has made a lasting impression on me, as a mentor, leader, and model, is Duane Webster, Executive Director of the Association of Research Libraries (ARL). Duane will retire in May 2008 after thirty-eight years of service and his presence will be greatly missed.

I first met Duane Webster in 1973 when I was Associate Director of Libraries at the University of Rochester working on a Management Review and Analysis Program (MRAP) project. Duane was then working in ARL's Office of Management Studies and was serving as a consultant to the University of Rochester Libraries for its MRAP study. I was immediately impressed with his professional knowledge and understanding of library issues and, most of all, his vision for libraries of the future. I later became better acquainted with him when I had an opportunity to serve on the committee that oversaw the Office of Management Studies.

When I became Dean of University Libraries at the University of Oklahoma in 1978, my work brought me in more frequent contact with Duane. As I began my new position at Oklahoma, the University Libraries was finishing its own MRAP study and I invited Duane to speak to the librarians here. In 1988, he became Executive Director of the Association of Research Libraries, and our already lengthy association continued and our friendship grew.

---

Sul H. Lee, Peggy V. Helmerich Chair, Dean of University Libraries, Professor of Bibliography, and Professor of Library and Information Studies, The University of Oklahoma, Norman, OK.

Duane was executive director of ARL for twenty years. That in itself is a major accomplishment. It is the longest tenure of an executive director in ARL's history and speaks volumes about Duane's interpersonal and leadership skills. It is, indeed, a challenge to lead 123 of North America's most accomplished librarians for two decades.

It was Duane's leadership that brought a new era to ARL beginning in 1989 as he addressed a wide variety of emerging issues in ways that positively affected all academic libraries. Duane created the ARL Office of Scholarly Communication, which called attention to skyrocketing serial prices and explored ways and means of dealing with this financial crisis in libraries. In partnership with CAUSE he established the Coalition for Networked Information (CNI), which promoted the use of the Internet to enhance academic scholarship. He has played a major role in its development, management, and staffing over the years. It was under his leadership that ARL secured a grant from the Andrew W. Mellon Foundation to put in place a professionally staffed unit for gathering statistics and measurement capacity to improve ARL data. Working with Texas A&M University staff, Duane developed web-based assessment services that allowed universities to analyze and evaluate user perceptions of library performance. This service became known as LibQUAL+ and has been utilized by many academic libraries to improve services for their clientele. He began the Scholarly Publishing and Academic Resources Coalition (SPARC) to promote scholarly publishing systems for the improvement of access to scholarly journals in the sciences, technology, and medicine.

Equally important was Duane's establishment of the Global Resources Network for improving access to foreign language resources and his work with intellectual property legislation and litigation. He was in the forefront to promote a diversity program that helped research libraries build a more diverse staff, and he was a strong advocate for enhanced copyright legislation. Indeed, Duane was a key player in the development of the Library Copyright Alliance.

A couple of Duane's accomplishments were tangential to his work with library issues, but nonetheless of paramount importance to the ARL. One was his successful increase of the ARL organizational budget from $3 million to more than $7 million and the establishment of a $1 million reserve fund. Another achievement was moving the organization to 21 DuPont Circle, which made the ARL more visible to its constituency and improved the working space for its staff. His efforts to make ARL an integral part of higher education were rewarded in partnerships with

EDUCAUSE and the establishment of CNI; with the Association of American Universities (AAU) and the creation of Global Resources Network; and, perhaps most significantly, the invitation for ARL to join and become the only library-related organization in the Washington Higher Education Secretariat.

From another perspective, but highly indicative of his dedication to his work, it should be noted that in the thirty-eight years of his association with ARL, Duane never missed a membership meeting and participated in more than two hundred ARL board meetings. During this time he has worked with more than 500 ARL member representatives and reported to nineteen different ARL presidents.

Duane's career with ARL may be summed up by noting that he successfully raised the influence and visibility of the organization both nationally and internationally and while doing so improved scholarly communication and focused attention on the rapidly changing role of the academic library. These are all laudable achievements that reflect Duane's amazing leadership abilities. I predict it will be a long time before his achievements are equaled and even longer before they are surpassed. Thanks to Duane Webster, ARL has become a more responsive and more effective organization. It has become an organization synonymous with excellence. I know that I speak for many colleagues both in and outside of ARL when I say Duane Webster will be missed greatly by the profession. Thank you, Duane, for the service you have given to research libraries.

*This tribute will be published as an editorial in a forthcoming issue of Journal of Library Administration*

# Local to Global: The Emerging Research Library

Lizabeth A. Wilson

**ABSTRACT.** Research, scholarship, and discovery have been transformed by the internet and communication technologies across all sectors on a global basis. The rapid dissemination of findings, the creation of new tools and platforms for information manipulation, and open access to research data have rendered the more traditional institution-based library approaches to providing access to information inadequate. This paper will examine collective choices and strategies needed to move local collections and services to a global scale in the emerging research library.

## *LOOKING BACK AND LOOKING FORWARD*

A look to the past is always a good place to start when envisioning the future. Early in the last century, Henry Suzzallo was the president of the University of Washington (UW), a fledgling institution in a rainy wilderness called Seattle. President Suzzallo's vision was to build a "university of a thousand years."

He knew that all great universities had great libraries. His first action was to create a library to rival those in Europe. He called it a "cathedral of books." Up from the empty land, arose a grand gothic structure with the

---

Lizabeth A. Wilson is Dean of University Libraries, University of Washington, Seattle, WA.

Olympic Mountains and the Pacific Ocean off in the distance. Suzzallo's "university of a thousand years" had its cathedral.

Since then, the Suzzallo Library has become known as the "the soul of the university" and is a beloved symbol for Huskies around the world. Unfortunately, Suzzallo's "cathedral of books" ultimately would get him fired for having aspirations that the then governor of Washington viewed as foolish and extravagant.

President Suzzallo knew what the twentieth-century library should be—a magnificent building of inspirational architecture filled with the finest books from all around the world. Suzzallo had a clear vision. Fast forward to today and one thing remains the same. The future of the university is inseparable from the future of the library. James Duderstadt, president *emeritus* of the University of Michigan, has said that the library of the future may in fact *predict* the future of the university.

The networked environment and the accelerated pace of change have transformed libraries and higher education. Easy-to-use search engines providing access to a vast array of content have changed our daily information-seeking behavior and expectations. Significant opportunities now exist to create digital content from our stacks and make widely available what had once been hidden in our special collections. Libraries have been reshaped into flexible learning spaces to meet a variety of user needs—collaborative and individual study, hi-tech, hi-touch instruction, and caffeine and chatter.

Libraries and librarians have been persistent agents of change and reflection. We have been innovative and creative, and have brought technology into the service of learning and research. In many ways, we have collectively put the twentieth-century library of Henry Suzzallo out of business. We cannot fully articulate the shape of the twenty-first-century library, but we do know it will not be merely a "cathedral of books."

Our future will be determined in large part by how we collectively respond to the networked world and anytime/anyplace expectations. Education and research demands a complex, integrated, and increasingly global information infrastructure. Universities will be measured by how well they disseminate knowledge. Universities will need to find new ways to share intellectual effort in order to advance discovery and educate students for a future we cannot even begin to imagine.

Yet during this transformation, the mission of the library will remain constant—to meet the information needs of the community through the selection, organization, preservation, creation, and dissemination of information and knowledge. The tactics and strategies have and will continue to change. Like my fellow library directors around the globe, I grapple with the shape and form of the emerging library every day. I ask:

- What do faculty and students value? What will the scholar in 2050 expect us to have selected and preserved—blogs, mash-ups, research data?
- How can we support the expanding university mission in a technology-enabled world?
- Where should we invest when we have limited resources, conflicting priorities, proliferating publics, and often competing clientele?

## PREFERRED FUTURES

When it comes to making predictions about the future, a wise person once said that "those who make crystal ball predictions often end up eating glass." At the risk of getting shards between my teeth, I will speculate about the emerging research library. What do I see in my crystal ball? I see many futures swirling around, and my preferred future is inherently and fundamentally global.

In my preferred future, faculty, students, and researchers can access and use the information they require when and where they want it around the world and in the format most appropriate to their needs. Better yet, make that a future where libraries anticipate their needs and are woven into the fabric of the search for knowledge and into the flow of discovery and research. I envision a future in which our physical and virtual libraries are trusted and robust, and engender human understanding. I envision a transformed scholarly communication system that is both accessible and affordable, regardless of where one lives on the globe or one's institutional affiliation. I envision digital libraries that have reached their potential to improve research productivity and facilitate deep learning. I envision a future in which our faculty and students will be as information fluent as they are reading and writing literate and technology competent.

Guided by *Vision 2010*, we are working on that future at UW.[1] *Vision 2010* describes aspirations that are steeped in the local with a reach to the global: "The University of Washington Libraries is an international leader in imagining, creating, and realizing the promise of the 21st century academic research library. As the intellectual and physical commons of our great University, we advance discovery and encourage the growth of knowledge. We anticipate and meet the information needs of our diverse communities, at any time and in any place. We prepare students for success in life as information smart global citizens."

We require a global research library that is not defined by institutional parameters or geographic location if we are to advance the work of twenty-first-century universities and colleges. I would like to suggest four strategies worth our collective investment as we shape this emerging research library.

1. Collaboration.
2. Building a culture of assessment.
3. The global research library.
4. Moving to the network (global) level.

## *COLLABORATION*

The transformative research library is only possible through collaboration. Collaboration and collective action will be defining characteristics of the twenty-first-century library. We can no longer feel complacent about the artificial boundaries among our libraries. The most urgent issues—scholarly communication, digital libraries, and information literacy—require the contributions of many.

Libraries around the world will be even more interdependent and intertwined than ever before—not just with each other but with stakeholders, information providers, knowledge creators, and users. This will require a new cross-sector and global orientation. We must move as much as we can, in the parlance of Lorcan Dempsey, to the "network level."[2] We must do only at the local level what cannot be done collectively or does not make sense to be done at the global level.

Collaboration is needed to reframe scholarly publishing and dissemination. Collaboration is fundamental to a digital library that has purpose and value. Collaboration will help us engender an information-smart global community, which I am convinced is a precondition for a saner and more secure world.

Collaboration is not simply desirable, it is imperative. In all but the rarest of cases, one is too small a number to solve problems. As one sage said, "None of us is as smart as all of us." Collaboration is a choice. It cannot be mandated. It is hard work. It is fragile.

Collaboration does not come naturally. Collaboration is different from cooperation or coordination in vision and relationships; structure;

authority and accountability; resources and rewards; and people.³ Budget structures, administrative lines, and reward systems can create barriers to collaboration.

Collaborators learn how to cross boundaries and have a high tolerance for ambiguity. Innovative organizations pay attention to supporting the skills and providing the latitude needed in collaborations. Successful collaborations are based on people but are not dependent on a single personality. Many who have engaged in successful collaborations will tell you that collaboration is its own reward. Given a problem that the whole organization needs solved and a chance to do it well, individuals in collaborations will work for no more reward than the one they give themselves.

## CULTURE OF ASSESSMENT

When we think about the culture of libraries, we can conjure up many images: the culture of the book, the culture of knowledge, the culture of control, the culture of equal access, the culture of detail, the culture of community, the culture of memory, the culture of technology, or the culture of change. I ask that you think about libraries within a culture of assessment.⁴

What is a culture of assessment and why is it important to the future? A culture of assessment is an environment in which decisions are based on facts, research, and analysis, and where services are planned and delivered in ways that maximize positive outcomes and impacts for library clients. A culture of assessment is an integral part of the process of change and the creation of the twenty-first-century research library.

In our environment of continual change and new opportunities, we need to focus explicitly on the user. We must invest in continuously assessing the landscape, listening to our users, and looking for places where we can make a difference in connecting people with knowledge.

In the early '90s under the directorship of Betty Bengtson, the University of Washington Libraries made a commitment to become a user-centered enterprise. We explicitly defined who our users were in order to determine if we were meeting their needs. We positioned ourselves to make the best use of resources, to select the best from a growing array of options, and to market services realistically. Most importantly, we engaged both staff and users in a decision-making dialog on what new services, collections, information formats, and programs would be introduced and what we would no longer do or provide.

A decade later, we continue to nurture our culture of assessment and dedicate significant resources to gathering and mining robust data about users and their information needs. Triennial surveys, begun in 1992, provide invaluable information about students' and faculty's needs and priorities, and the importance of and satisfaction with the libraries during a period of unprecedented change. We actively listen to our users through surveys, usability testing, environmental scanning, LibQUAL, focus groups, and learning outcomes, and do something with what we learn.[5] What have we learned?

- In general, the triennial surveys show that faculty and students are moving rapidly toward remote use of online information. Indeed, it is the preferred method for finding and using information needed for work.
- Self-reliance and the ability to perform library-related work without staff mediation are of high importance to our users.
- Information technology and online information resources have enabled faculty and students to be more productive.
- Across all groups (faculty as well as graduate and undergraduate students), desktop delivery of full-text resources ranked as the highest priority.
- For undergraduates, *place* is very important.

Our physical facilities are used extensively by students who account for more than 90 percent of the 4.4 million annual visits. Undergraduates use the library as their primary space for library research, course work, individual study, socializing, and group work and presentations. The library is the largest and most important learning space at the university, and it is open twenty-four hours a day.

As an example of our focus group work, we worked to understand the information needs of the burgeoning number of bioscientists and to figure out how to better serve them.[6] What did we learn from the bioscience focus groups?

- Everyone wants more electronic access. For these individuals, print is dead, really dead.
- The library is seen primarily as an e-journal provider with a big check book.
- Most bioscience faculty do not come to the physical library but use the virtual library more than ever.

- Most graduate and undergraduate students come to the physical library as a place to work.
- Article databases, except *Web of Science*, are underused.
- There is a great need for personal information management.
- Most faculty members with grant support buy what books they need from Amazon.com because it delivers to their offices.
- The transaction cost from discovery to delivery is too high, particularly in time and lost opportunity. There is a need to integrate fragmented systems and processes.
- Bioscience researchers are multidisciplinary and multi-institutional collaborators. They work with people within UW, across the nation, and around the globe.
- They are everywhere, in scattered locations. The department is simply a place holder where they pick up their checks.
- Bioscience researchers are independent and self-sufficient; they rely on external funding for their existence. They are, in the parlance of baseball, free agents.

These findings have profound implications for library strategies and where to invest for one segment of our diverse clientele. We use our fifteen years of data on user behavior and priorities to make better decisions, allocate and reallocate resources, improve services, and create a preferred future. As the Dean of the Libraries, everyday I draw on our assessment work to communicate our impact, resource needs, and new capacities. Assessment gives library directors tools for advocacy and insight into the emerging research library. I cannot imagine being an effective, or responsible, library leader without our assessment program. That would be like walking a tightrope without a net—initially exciting but ultimately foolish.

## *GLOBAL RESEARCH LIBRARY*

Scholarship and discovery is increasingly global and multidisciplinary. One researcher told me that she works with collaborators in five countries and in more than ten institutions. Researchers are challenged to manage the vast amounts of data they are generating. Many are suffering from an overwhelming amount of information, demands of immediacy, and management of expectations. The world of research and discovery, and thus libraries, has changed fundamentally—with all of the inherent risks, opportunities, and impediments that come along with such profound change.

Depending on our collective choices, I believe the role of the research library in 2020 could span a continuum of marginal to transformational. But there are many questions to answer.

- How would we go about creating this global research library?
- What does it mean to be global?
- What does a global cyberinfrastructure entail?
- What are the elements of the global regulatory and policy framework?
- What are the implications for the libraries workforce?

Some like-minded souls began batting around these questions, and the Global Research Library 2020 (GRL2020) was born.[7] The University of Washington Libraries and Microsoft Corporation jointly convened GRL2020 in Woodinville, Washington, September 30 through October 2, 2007. GRL2020 seeks to create a roadmap for the global research library by bringing together a select group of global leaders from different sectors to engage in three days of intensive discussions and presentations. Attendees traveled from Europe, China, India, Japan, Canada, Australia, and all over the United States to participate in the workshop.

Tony Hey of Microsoft Technical Computing joined me in setting the stage. Tony and I agreed that in order for research libraries to play a central role in this increasingly multi-institutional and cross-sector environment, they must find new approaches for how they operate, and add value to research and discovery on a global basis. The opening discussions focused on a wide array of issues related to understanding the output of global research. Many global grand challenges (e.g., climate change, global health, and economic issues) require support for the research enterprise that transcends political boundaries, and provides a new infrastructure and cooperative framework.

Participants largely agreed on core value propositions for the Global Research Library:

- Innovation and knowledge creation rely on sustained availability of information.
- The creation of public value is central to the mission of global research libraries.

- Selection, sharing, and sustainability are longstanding components of library missions, and remain so as library assets transition from paper to digital formats.
- Long-term curation of content is critical, and requires focused effort in the development of systems and standards to support them in the long digital future ahead.

Most agreed that the global research library of the future will be an interoperable network of services, resources, and expertise designed to facilitate the process of research and the selecting, sharing, and sustaining of the outputs of research. Infrastructure was broadly interpreted to include telecommunications, protocol standards, computing, electronic publishing, repositories, discovery and delivery services, and instructional services necessary to support rapidly changing skills that support these technologies. The current state of overlapping infrastructures must be integrated and managed within policy frameworks by staff with appropriate skills now uncommon in the profession. If the interoperable components of such infrastructure can be agreed upon and shared, many were hopeful that the costs of the enterprise could be reduced and efficiencies increased.

The growing worldwide trend toward Open Access was a focal point of attention. Open models of scholarly publication and research are recognized as a key to improving the effectiveness of research and learning in the developing, as well as the developed, world. Research libraries would due well to exploit Web 2.0 capabilities to engender cross-sector structures where public, private, and governmental agencies may find shared purpose and mutual benefit.

The GRL2020 group outlined critical impediments that must be addressed if the vision of the global research library of the future is to be realized:

- Funding for research and learning is fragmented and suffers from steep disparities globally.
- Intellectual Property and copyright constraints increase friction in the information supply chain.
- Complexity of the stakeholder environment impairs interoperability and information flow.
- Cross-sector tensions and proprietary perspectives dilute resources and leadership.
- Infrastructure deficiencies, especially in developing countries, limit the scope and effectiveness of recognized solutions.

- Economic and technological sustainability are problems at all levels.
- Skills appropriate to the twenty-first-century information world are scarce in our current twentieth-century workforce.
- Disparate political, economic, and cultural environments can create barriers to meaningful collaboration.

The Italian National Research Council's Institute of Information Science and Technologies (CNR-ITSI) hosted the follow-up workshop March 27–28, 2008, in Pisa, and a summary of those deliberations also can be found on the GRL 2020 Web site.

## *MOVING TO THE NETWORK (GLOBAL) LEVEL*

The fourth and final area for investment grows out of Dempsey's admonition to libraries to examine what we should do at the network level that we no longer need to do at the local level. What can a local library do to help build the global research library? The University of Washington Libraries is partnering with OCLC to move local "discovery and delivery" to a global scale through WorldCat Local.[8]

Through OCLC WorldCat.org, a user can find resources in WorldCat through the open Web and then click back to a local library. Through WorldCat Local, we are testing global content, a localized version of WorldCat.org, and interoperability with local services such as circulation, interlibrary loan, and online full-text resources.

UW's local manifestation of WorldCat.org provides local branding, custom ranking, full functionality, article metadata, and faceted browsing. Results are presented from UW first, then our regional consortium (Orbis Cascade Alliance), and then the world. The user can directly request the item, regardless of format or location in the world, by linking to the local delivery systems (e.g., Illiad, Innovative, electronic full-text, etc.).

WorldCat Local provides a global platform, access to the global network, and syndication across the globe. It also allows an individual library to operate at the global scale—a defining characteristic of twenty-first-century research, teaching, and learning.

## *A STORY OF GLOBAL PROPORTIONS*

I promised that I would end with a story. This is a story about how local research libraries can change lives through the convergence of people, ideas, and global connections. It is a story about connecting people with knowledge to advance discovery and improve their quality of life.

This story begins with a computer science project, winds its way through the library, and ends up in Peru. The year is 2003. The place is UW. The student is named Zach.[9]

In many ways Zach is a typical freshman. He is a double major in math and Spanish; interested in dating, movies and music; downs coffee by the mug; and parties regularly with his friends. He loves the outdoors. He lists cross-country skiing, mountain biking, and hiking as his favorite hobbies. And, Zach has been blind since birth.

Zach says, "I don't think many people fully understand the implication of not being able to 'see' a mathematical figure on how one understands a discipline." As a sophomore, Zach joined a multidisciplinary team on the Tactile Graphics Project funded by the National Science Foundation.[10] The team crafted software for the rapid translation of graphical images into a form similar to Braille.

This project made many things possible for Zach. It reduced the time necessary to translate a single mathematical graphic from a textbook into tactile form. Zach says that the Tactile Graphics Project saved his college career. Zach believes he could not have majored in math anywhere but UW.

Zach also majored in Spanish, and this is where his story takes a turn through the library stacks. Two years ago, Zach was researching a paper on Quechua for a Spanish linguistics class. Quechua is the language of the ancient Inca Empire and is spoken today in various dialects by ten million indigenous people throughout South America.

Zach found a footnote on the Internet concerning a linguist who did groundbreaking work in the 1960s. Even though he could not find much of substance to write a decent paper, he was determined to learn more about the language and this man named Alfredo Torrero, the father of Andean linguistics.

He headed over to the Odegaard Undergraduate Library and found librarian Laura Barrett. Laura worked her magic. She led Zach through a multilingual and multinational labyrinth of scholarly indexes and citations until they picked up some promising leads.

Because of our partnership with libraries around the world, Zach was able to physically put his hands on the rare and elusive books and articles. One book came from Utah, another from Michigan, and several from Peru. Zach scanned as many as he could and continued to devour them in Braille even after he had turned in his paper. Each time he read Torrero, he felt like he was discovering something completely new. He knew he was, in some instances, the first person in North America to read Torrero's books and definitely the first person to read them in Braille. He became enchanted with the Quechua language and Torrero.

After graduation, Zach boarded a plane for Peru to live, teach, and study Quechua. He is working with a scholar who once studied with the late Torrero. He plans to help a team of University of San Marcos computer scientists and linguists design a Braille system for Quechua. Quechuans who are blind will be able to do something they have never done before—read their own language.

In the library, Zach found his passion, and his path was altered forever. The Quechuans with whom Zach is working will probably never have the opportunity to visit UW and ask a question of someone like Laura Barrett. However, their lives have been changed forever by a student named Zach and libraries half a world away.

Universities and colleges have many stories to tell—stories that inspire, stories that reach around the globe. Many of these stories begin or end in a library. Without a collective contribution to building global research libraries that connect people with knowledge, there would be no story.

## *FINAL THOUGHTS*

This paper started with Suzzallo's vision of a cathedral of books, and it is an appropriate place to end. Our generation is not the first to wrestle with the shape of the emerging research library. While much is uncertain, I am confident that the emerging research library will be:

- both virtual and real,
- flexible and networked,
- multidimensional and integrated, and
- part of a library ecosystem sustained through collaboration.

Above all, the emerging research library will be defined by its ability to move effortlessly from local to global and back again.

### NOTES

1. University of Washington Libraries. "*Vision 2010*," http://www.lib.washington.edu/about/vision2010/ (accessed June 23, 2008).
2. Dempsey, Lorcan. "Libraries and the Long Tail: Some Thoughts about Libraries in a Network Age." *D-Lib Magazine* (April 2006). http://www.dlib.org/dlib/april06/dempsey/04dempsey.html (accessed June 23, 2008).

3. For further discussion on lessons learned, see Mattessich, Paul. *Collaboration—What Makes It Work: A Review of Research Literature on Factors Influencing Successful Collaboration* (St. Paul, MN: Amherst H. Wilder Foundation, 1992); and Shepard, Murray, Virginia Gillham, and Michael Ridley. "The Truth Is in the Details: Lessons in Inter-University Library Collaboration." *Library Management* (1999): 332–37.

4. Steve Hiller, University of Washington Libraries, first used the phrase "culture of assessment" in 1994. He was inspired by Robert Hughes's *Culture of Complain: The Fraying of America* (New York: Oxford University Press, 1993).

5. University of Washington Libraries Assessment. http://www.lib.washington.edu/assessment/ (accessed June 23, 2008).

6. University of Washington Libraries Biosciences Taskforce. (2007). http://www.lib.washington.edu/assessment/reports/ (accessed June 23, 2008).

7. This section draws from the workshop summary crafted by Stuart Weibel and Ann Ferguson available on the Global Research Library 2020 Web site. http://www.grl2020.net (accessed June 23, 2008). A similar summary was also published in *Futures: Microsoft's European Innovation Magazine* (December 2007) (accessed June 23, 2008).

8. WorldCat Local. (2008). http://www.oclc.org/worldcatlocal/ (accessed June 23, 2008).

9. Portions of this story are based on an article by Jamie Hale entitled "Tactile Graphics Help Visually Impaired Students." *The Daily of the University of Washington* (February 22, 2005). http://thedaily.washington.edu/2005/2/22/tactile-graphics-help-visually-impaired-students/ (accessed June 23, 2008). Other details provided in a personal e-mail transmission from Zach to librarian Laura Barrett.

10. Tactile Graphics Project. (2008). http://tactilegraphics.cs.washington.edu/ (accessed June 23, 2008).

# Partners in Knowledge Creation: An Expanded Role for Research Libraries in the Digital Future

Mary M. Case

**ABSTRACT.** Libraries have always been involved in the creation of new knowledge by ensuring that the knowledge of the past is collected, organized, made accessible and preserved for coming generations. The digital world provides the opportunity for librarians to be even more actively engaged in the creation process. These new roles range from the creation of metadata to the development of repositories to the publication of scholarly work. By integrating the skills and values of librarians with the work of scholars and the expertise of technologists can we ensure long-term access to scholarship and the continued relevance of libraries.

## INTRODUCTION

Academic libraries and faculty are natural partners in the expanding role of the research library in the digital future. Academic librarians have always worked closely with faculty who are our primary constituency. It is faculty whose research interests drive a great portion of our collecting; in fact, it is the faculty who built our collections for many years.

---

Mary M. Case, A.M.L.S., is University Librarian and Professor, University of Illinois at Chicago, 801 South Morgan Street, Chicago, IL 60607 (E-mail: marycase@uic.edu).

Over the years, libraries have also assisted faculty by providing a number of bibliographic services. Librarians have been asked to check citations of dissertations or journal manuscripts that faculty are reviewing. In the pre-Web world, librarians conducted mediated searches of databases, using our expertise in constructing search strategies and understanding of controlled vocabularies. Many reference librarians have spent hours tracking down garbled citations and identifying the one library that could provide a resource through interlibrary loan.

Some faculty have even developed close working relationships with staff in special collections, archives, and other units holding "hidden collections" where the knowledge of the staff is critical to unearthing hidden treasures. Increasingly, faculty have turned to librarians to provide personal and classroom instruction in navigating the literatures of their own or related fields.

Libraries have provided and continue to provide assistance to faculty during the knowledge creation process, yet the underlying functions that support these services have remained almost invisible (selection, acquisitions, cataloging, access, preservation, online systems development, and digitization); unless, of course, something goes wrong (Why don't you have this book? Why is the book I ordered not here yet? This book is classified in the wrong place. Why is this work only available on microfilm? Why is the system so slow?). It is this expertise, often found in the backrooms of our libraries, that is in growing demand by faculty in the digital age. And it is this expertise that provides librarians with the opportunity to engage directly with faculty in their research, teaching, and professional activities in a way qualitatively different from and rarely possible before.

## *FACULTY AND THE DIGITAL AGE*

As faculty engage the digital world, they find themselves creating a variety of products as a part of their research and teaching. These include databases, online learning modules, online journals, and topical Web sites, to name a few. As faculty work with these products, they begin to face the questions of selection, copyright, organization and access, structures and vocabularies, and even long-term accessibility; many have sought out librarians to help them sort through these issues. They recognize that having developed and implemented online integrated systems over the past thirty years and having created or licensed significant amounts of digital information over the past fifteen, librarians have developed an expertise in managing digital resources.

In the last couple of years at my own institution, librarians have received requests from faculty for help in a number of these areas. The following are just a few examples. I suspect what is happening at our institution is no different than what is happening at most universities today.

- A young mathematician who places all of his work on his personal Web site and rarely publishes in journals is eager to have an institutional home for his articles to ensure their longevity. He is intrigued by the notion that metadata might increase the likelihood that his work will be found.
- A behavioral scientist in social work is editor-in-chief of an open access journal and thought the library might serve as an archival home for his work. The Library was considering implementing an open source publishing system and proposed to host the journal, hoping that we may be able to reduce the production costs in addition to providing an archival home.
- A faculty member in bioinformatics and his research colleagues had numerous data files for which they needed a permanent home so the data files could be cited and readily accessed by others.
- A faculty member involved with work in 3-D visualization sees the library as the logical entity to archive these programs.
- One of our health sciences colleges is reworking its entire curriculum to provide all course content (syllabi, lectures, faculty notes, images, articles, books) through the campus's learning management system. The college has asked the library for help in assessing copyright and licensing issues, in creating metadata for the vast array of images and articles to be included, and in identifying additional relevant book resources available in digital form.
- The Director of Research in the College of Medicine's Department of Medical Education has asked for a librarian to serve as co-Principal Investigator on a grant to develop a dataset repository in medical education research. Metadata schemes and controlled vocabularies are key components of the proposal.
- Hearing about our institutional repository, a faculty member in history approached us about digitizing and posting online his out-of-print book about trials in the late Roman Republic.
- As a part of a grant, a faculty member in public health wanted to create an open access journal to publish the results of his and his

colleagues' research. The faculty member thought the Library would be the ideal home for such a journal and asked for a proposal. While the grant was not funded, the faculty member has recently decided that he would nonetheless like to start the journal.

While the library has not yet been able to accommodate all of these requests (and in some cases, may never be able to do so), they are indicative of the opportunities that abound in this current environment. We are, however, at what I believe to be a critical point. The faculty believe that we have skills that are of direct value to the work they are doing. If we are not prepared to respond by providing consulting, project management, technical support, or a permanent project home, the faculty will turn elsewhere. Some other entity will provide these services. If that is the case, we will have lost the opportunity to work in partnership with faculty in the creation of new knowledge and perhaps even in the development of new forms of scholarly publishing.

## *IMPORTANCE OF LIBRARY PARTICIPATION*

At a time when we see fewer and fewer faculty in our physical facilities, it is heartening to realize that many of them recognize the relevance of the library to the new knowledge they are creating through research, publishing, and teaching. As highlighted in the examples above, they are reaching out to us to provide guidance with metadata structures and controlled vocabularies, copyright issues, and preservation solutions, but why is it so critical for librarians to respond? In addition to information management skills we can contribute, librarians bring a set of values that are fundamental to the long-term survival of scholarship.

Librarians care about access. They understand that resources may have value to disciplines and time periods well beyond those for which the resources were initially intended. They understand that the sooner a database or research finding is made openly available, the sooner it can inform other studies, change practice, and influence policy. They understand not only the need to respect the rights of copyright owners when using others' work, but also the intent of fair use and how researchers can manage their own copyrights to maximize the impact of their work. Librarians understand that in the digital world, issues of long-term access and preservation need to be addressed directly at the beginning of the creative process.

All this has an impact on the choices of structures, formats, metadata schemes, vocabularies, access and use policies, and ultimate disposition of a faculty member's digital works. By being involved in these choices, librarians can help faculty make the decisions that will increase the odds that valuable scholarship in digital form will not be lost. In fact, our goal should be to help make this scholarship easily found, readily used, and permanently preserved.

By being directly engaged with faculty on these issues, librarians also have the opportunity to build the expertise and infrastructure that can solidify their role in the evolving future of digital scholarship. Several recent reports and program announcements—including the National Science Foundation (NSF) and American Council of Learned Societies' reports on cyberinfrastructure,[1] the NSF Datanet grant program,[2] the Ithaka report on university publishing,[3] and the Shulenburger article[4] on university distribution strategies—all envision a role in this effort for librarians working in partnership with domain experts and computer and information scientists, among others.

In the end, we must be understood as essential partners in knowledge creation. If we remain the distant providers of electronic resources and the occasional instructor in the classroom, we run the risk of losing faculty support in tight budget times. Many of us have had the experience of deans or faculty questioning why they should be supporting such central services as the library. We must be visible; we must be at the table—both for the sake of the long-term survival of digital scholarship and of ourselves.

## *METADATA & DIGITIZATION SERVICES*

In a recent article,[5] G. Sayeed Choudhury of Johns Hopkins University Library describes quite eloquently the impact of the librarian-faculty partnership. Choudhury discusses the interaction of the library's Digital Research and Curation Center (DRCC) with Hopkins' astronomers in the creation of the Virtual Observatory (VO). The VO is a project intended to "support new science by greatly enhancing access to data and computing resources, providing a 'virtual sky' and making it possible for astronomical researchers to find, retrieve, and analyze astronomical data from ground- and space-based telescopes worldwide."[6] The essence of the VO, according to Choudhury, is "*interoperability*. Data discovery, data access, and database queries are enabled by metadata standards."[7] He then goes on to explain how the project and partnership evolved:

In the process of getting to know each other, the librarians and astronomers moved the conversation further back in the data-curation process, from system design to reconsidering requirements. As we in the DRCC learned more about astronomy, we refined our suggestions about access mechanisms; as the astronomers of the VO learned more about digital archiving, they refined their suggestions about characteristics of curation. Essentially, we have started to make decisions about requirements, system design, implementation, sustainability, and governance together. There is no doubt that each group possesses specific expertise, and the growing understanding of each other's domains has resulted in unforeseen insights and a richer, collaborative decision-making process.[8]

Choudhury acknowledges that "the DRCC comprises a unique set of information technology professionals in a library setting who have conducted research and development for over 10 years."[9] Not all of us are fortunate to have the depth of expertise that Hopkins has in its Digital Research and Curation Center nor will we find ourselves involved (at least not yet) in such a large-scale project. Nevertheless, we are being asked by our faculty to provide a variety of services directly related to our skills in information management, metadata, copyright, preservation, and access. Our ability to respond can lead to productive partnerships and better results.

Libraries do seem to be responding to faculty demand for help with digital initiatives. According to a recent Association of Research Libraries (ARL) SPEC Kit on Metadata, thirty-six or about 80 percent of the responding libraries indicated that their metadata librarians have responsibility for collaborating with partners both within and outside their institutions.[10] For example, Cornell University Library, as a part of its larger Digital Consulting & Production Services (DCAPS),[11] provides metadata services to university departments, journal publishers, libraries, and other organizations. The Metadata Services unit itself is located within the library's Technical Services division and offers support for: "Development of metadata & schemas; Design of data model and access; Consulting on metadata; and Production of metadata."[12] The Center for Digital Initiatives at Brown also provides metadata services as a part of a larger overall program.[13]

In addition to metadata, both Cornell and Brown are providing digitizing services and Web site design to faculty to support their teaching and research. While some of these projects may address short-term needs and be of limited appeal, others may lead to significant projects that could attract external funding or multi-institution participation. How these projects are conceived, designed, and implemented will have a profound impact on the ultimate value of the resource.

Providing metadata or digitization services to faculty is not without its challenges. The respondents in the ARL SPEC Kit on Metadata mentioned several of them, including the difficulty of managing projects that cross multiple units in the library and the campus, the proliferation of formats and standards posing significant problems for interoperability, and the difficulty of finding skilled individuals to serve as metadata specialists.[14]

## *DIGITAL REPOSITORIES*

Just a few weeks ago, the faculty of Arts and Sciences at Harvard University approved a strategy for ensuring wide distribution of its scholarship.[15] The new policy will require affected Harvard faculty to retain rights that would allow them to grant Harvard a nonexclusive license to use their articles in any noncommercial way to promote access. The primary vehicle at this point will be deposit of the final form of scholarly articles in the university's open access institutional repository (IR). A faculty member must request in writing a waiver from the policy for a particular work.[16] While the details are still to be worked out, this action by a major elite university could reinvigorate the discussion of repositories and increase the deposit rate at IRs around the country.

Over the last several years, libraries have actively embraced institutional repositories as important avenues for the distribution and preservation of campus digital assets. In a 2006 survey, 78 percent of ARL libraries responding had either implemented or were planning to implement a repository by the end of 2007.[17] Another broader census conducted in 2006 by researchers at the University of Michigan,[18] revealed that IRs were not just a research library phenomenon. About 22 percent of doctoral institutions, 18 percent of master's level institutions, and 12 percent of baccalaureate institutions responding had reported that they had implemented or were planning and pilot testing an IR.[19] The authors of the Michigan report also noted that among the 52 percent of the responding institutions who indicated that they were not currently planning an IR, about 50 percent reported that they were likely to begin planning within twenty-four months.[20]

Despite the enthusiasm of libraries, IRs have been slow to attract significant content from faculty. In both surveys mentioned above, recruiting content is among the top challenges reported by respondents. In the ARL survey, those who have implemented IRs "report a range of 20 objects to over 19,000."[21] The Michigan census reports "that an average IR bears about 4,100 digital documents representing about 30 document types."[22] To obtain these documents has required a number of strategies by libraries, including working with the early adopters, one-on-one conversations with faculty, presentations to groups, offers of library facilitation of the deposit, library monitoring of faculty publishing with follow-up to encourage rights retention and deposit, and library deposit of articles from journals where publishers have indicated their consent. Harvard is the first major U.S. institution to mandate deposit.

The article in the *Harvard Gazette*[23] announcing the results of the faculty vote articulates some of the key reasons libraries have persisted in their efforts to implement and populate repositories. Stuart Shieber, a professor of computer science who introduced the proposal, talks about the importance of the widest possible dissemination of Harvard's faculty's works for scholars around the world whose access has been restricted due to the high cost of journals. Shieber also notes that the Harvard action "should be a very powerful message to the academic community that we want and should have more control over how our work is used and disseminated."[24] In addition to increasing visibility of an institution's scholarship, providing free public access to that scholarship, and raising awareness of managing copyrights, other reasons for deploying repositories include the preservation of an institution's scholarly and administrative assets, responding to a faculty or administrative request for help with managing data, and exploring alternative vehicles for scholarly communication.[25]

Of particular interest and relevance to my theme are the findings of the Michigan study that examine "the role of the library as a viable partner in the research enterprise." The study found that about 50 percent of those who had implemented a repository rated this role as a more important benefit than they had anticipated when they were in the planning and pilot testing phase.[26] This suggests that having infrastructure in place and the ability to provide faculty an IR strategy can indeed help the library establish itself as a meaningful partner. Even if the repository in the end turns out not to be the solution for a particular project, the conversation itself—the interaction of the faculty and the library in mutual pursuit of a solution—creates a valuable partnership. Having a specific product in place—having thought about the issues and policies that impact use of a repository and the content—builds a level of expertise that allows that conversation to happen in the first place. It is through the conversations prompted by the repository and by a concrete faculty need that the issues librarians care so much about can come to the fore—access, copyright, preservation, findability, metadata, and so on. It is through these exchanges that we hope decisions will be made to deposit and preserve valuable scholarly content.

In addition to institutional repositories, however, libraries are also involved in various ways with disciplinary repositories. Some libraries, like Cornell with arXiv, are hosts of the repository. More frequently, libraries may be educators and facilitators. Perhaps uppermost on our minds at the moment is PubMed Central (PMC), the National Institutes of Health's (NIH) public access repository. Late last year, Congress passed legislation requiring recipients of NIH funding to deposit any articles resulting from their grants in PMC with public access to be granted no later than twelve months after publication.[27] This new policy, effective in April 2008, turns what was previously only a request to grantees into a mandate. Libraries across the country are working closely with their campus research and compliance officers to develop strategies to ensure that investigators and institutions fulfill their obligations under this policy. These discussions, as with those around local institutional repositories, will necessarily involve serious consideration of faculty management of copyrights. This is an opportunity to encourage faculty to retain not only rights to deposit their work in PMC, but also rights that will ensure their own subsequent use of their work along with deposit in the campus institutional repository.

Disciplinary repositories can also take the shape of massive datasets generated from fields that are heavily data driven. Astronomy is one such field and the VO project mentioned earlier in this article is one possible prototype of a data-curation system. Genbank for gene sequences, the Genome-Wide Association Studies data repository for genotype and phenotype data, and the Inter-University Consortium for Political and Social Research are additional examples of large-scale data repositories. How libraries can position themselves to play a role in this emerging world of e-science and e-scholarship has been the topic of a special task force of the Association of Research Libraries. In its recently released report,[28] the Task Force noted that while research libraries already possess the expertise needed to engage in e-science, their knowledge of the issues and current involvement is limited.[29] To remedy this, the report identifies strategies to build a better understanding of the issues within the research library community, along with strategies to raise awareness among the e-science stakeholders of the contributions libraries can make.[30] The potential impact of e-science is staggering—the Task Force believes it could be "transformational" for research libraries.[31] The next several years will be critical as libraries clarify and claim their role in e-science.

Potentially as transformative, another kind of repository on the horizon is one that will include the content from mass digitization projects. Neither disciplinary nor institutional, these repositories may come to include tens of millions of documents that cross multiple domains. For example, the library members of the Committee on Institutional Cooperation (CIC) agreed last year to develop a shared digital repository in which to deposit all of the content they will be receiving back from Google as a part of their mass digitization projects.[32] In addition to preserving the content and ensuring public access to that portion out of copyright, one of the great benefits of this project will be the development, in collaboration with faculty, of new tools to search, mine, and analyze this vast repository. The combination of large digital libraries with high-performance computing resources has come to be known as *cyberscholarship*. In a recent article on this topic, William Arms, Professor of Computer Science at Cornell University, notes: "Computer programs can identify latent patterns of information or relationships that will never be found by human searching and browsing."[33]

It is not clear whether a system of decentralized repositories will best serve the needs of research and scholarship in the future. Some believe that the demands of cyberscholarship and e-science will require the development of *superdata* centers.[34] I tend to believe there will be multiple layers of repositories with functions distributed and coordinated. In the meantime, however, through work with repositories, libraries today are creating opportunities to fulfill current researcher needs, broadening knowledge of copyright management, access and preservation issues, and building expertise that will help us contribute to the development of the repository systems of the future.

## *PUBLISHING*

Publishing is another activity in which libraries are heavily invested. Preliminary data from an ARL survey conducted in 2007 indicate that 44 percent (or 36) of the responding eighty-one libraries are engaged in publishing activities and another 21 percent (or 17) are developing such capabilities. Of those currently publishing, 88 percent are publishing journals and 71 percent are publishing monographs.[35] It is clear that many

ARL libraries envision publishing as an important new strategy in the digital environment.

Several of the early publishing initiatives launched by libraries were designed to help scientific, professional, and scholarly publishers migrate to the electronic environment cost-effectively. Stanford University Library's Highwire Press and Johns Hopkins University Project Muse are examples of large-scale successes in this category. Other projects were developed as responses to a dysfunctional scholarly publishing system. The eScholarship Publishing Program of the California Digital Library and the University of Michigan's Scholarly Publishing Office were established to work with faculty to explore innovative, technology-facilitated, cost-effective alternatives of making scholarship accessible.

Also established in response to a dysfunctional market, the Office of Digital Scholarly Publishing (ODSP) at Penn State is a joint enterprise between the library and the University Press. One of its first projects was to provide a cost-effective outlet for work in one of the humanities disciplines marginalized by decreased sales. *Penn State Romance Studies*, a monographic series discontinued by the Press as no longer economically viable, was reinstated by the ODSP as an online open access series with a print-on-demand option. Faculty members in two foreign language and literature departments serve as editorial board members soliciting and evaluating book proposals.[36]

Libraries are also supporting the exploration of new forms of digital scholarship and publishing. The University of Virginia Library has had a long history of working with scholars on "thematic research collections"[37] through its support of the Institute for Advanced Technology in the Humanities.[38] The Blake Archive, the Rossetti Archive, and the Valley of the Shadow are well-known examples. The Walt Whitman Archive, another Institute project, is now housed at the University of Nebraska's Center for Digital Research in the Humanities, codirected by a faculty member and a librarian.[39] Columbia University Library in collaboration with the American Historical Association and Columbia University Press has published a series of digital monographs meant to experiment with innovative uses of technology to create content and experiences not possible in printed works.[40] The University of California eScholarship Publishing Program is collaborating with scholars to produce a digital critical edition of Mark Twain's works using "innovative search, display and citation technology,"[41] but you need not be Columbia, California, Virginia, Johns Hopkins, or Michigan, or have a local university press with which to partner, to undertake a publishing program. With both open source software and commercially hosted solutions available, some level of activity is possible. Locally, we have implemented Open Journal Systems (OJS),[42] an open source journals management program and have three journals online. We have had conversations with and demonstrated OJS to many campus editors. Some have liked OJS so much that they decided to load their own copy to manage the receipt, reviewing and tracking of manuscripts with final publication handled by their original publisher. This is a positive outcome. The library has provided a service linked to one of the critical professional roles of faculty. Moreover, it provides an opportunity to open a conversation about editor contracts, journal prices, copyright, metadata, open access, and preservation.

## *IMPLICATIONS*

Embracing this role as engaged partners in the creation of knowledge, libraries will face a number of implications having to do with our staff, our organization, and our campus relationships. While it is true that libraries already have experience and skills in areas of interest to faculty, it is also true that we do not necessarily have the depth or breadth of expertise or the right person with the expertise. We may be able to manage for a while with motivated staff that we have been able to reallocate to support our repository and publishing initiatives (which we have done at UIC), but to expand our programs and be effective long-term partners with faculty, we must carefully consider and develop or hire professionals with the skills we need. As we look even further down the road at e-science and cyberscholarship, we may need entirely new kinds of staff. In his article, Choudhury notes that we will likely need what he calls "data scientists" in the future—individuals "who can act as human interfaces between libraries and domain experts."[43] These may be our next generation liaisons.

In addition to staff, however, we need to organize ourselves to be able to respond to requests from faculty in a coherent and consistent way. Locally, we are just beginning a process to identify how we can bring together disparate digital services to provide both efficient internal digitization capacity and external consulting and production services that would include not only metadata and digitization, but also our repository and publishing efforts. Both Cornell with their Digital Consulting & Production Services, and Brown with their Center for Digital Initiatives, though large institutions, may be models to investigate.

Another important aspect of our work with faculty is that we cannot do it alone. At the very least, we need to build on the relationships we have with our computing operations and our university presses, as appropriate. At UIC, we have had an informal relationship with our computing center, which provides the programming and server space for our installation of OJS. A number of libraries that have had such ad hoc arrangements with presses and information technology units have realized at some point in their evolution that more formalized structures were needed. The creation of the Electronic Publishing Initiative @ Columbia (EPIC) arose from the recognition that a formal organization with a focused mission that brought together skills from the library, press, and academic computing staffs would be needed to scale up production capabilities and develop partnerships more effectively.[44] The California Digital Library and the University of California Press recently announced that they would be formalizing their collaboration "to bring together their different strengths, increase the visibility of UC publishing activities, and institutionalize what has been up to now a series of experimental, ad hoc activities."[45]

No matter our size or complexity, issues of staff, organization, and institutionalized relationships will be critical to examine as our aspirations and faculty expectations grow.

## *CONCLUSION*

Partnering with faculty in the act of creating knowledge in the digital age is not only a tremendous opportunity for libraries, but ultimately an obligation. We owe it to the faculty to share our expertise to help make the products they create more valuable. We owe it to ourselves to build our expertise and secure the library's future as a significant partner in research and scholarship. Most importantly, we owe it to future scholars to ensure that the work of their predecessors is findable, accessible, and usable next year and next century.

## NOTES

1. National Science Foundation (NSF), *Revolutionizing Science and Engineering through Cyberinfrastructure: Report of the National Science Foundation Blue-Ribbon Advisory Panel on Cyberinfrastructure*, January 2003, http://www.nsf.gov/cise/sci/reports/atkins.pdf (accessed February 2, 2008); National Science Foundation Cyberinfrastructure Council, *Cyberinfrastructure Vision for 21st Century Discovery*,

March 2007, http://www.nsf.gov/od/oci/CI_Vision_March07.pdf (accessed February 2, 2008); American Council of Learned Societies, *Our Cultural Commonwealth: The Report of the American Council of Learned Societies Commission on Cyberinfrastructure for the Humanities and Social Sciences*, 2006, http://www.acls.org/cyberinfrastructure/OurCulturalCommonwealth.pdf (accessed February 2, 2008).

2. National Science Foundation, *Sustainable Digital Data Preservation and Access Network Partners (DataNet)*, Program Solicitation, NSF 07-601, http://www.nsf.gov/pubs/2007/nsf07601/nsf07601.htm (accessed November 19, 2007).

3. Brown, Laura, Griffiths, Rebecca, and Rascoff, Matthew, "University Publishing in a Digital Age," *Ithaka Report*, July 26, 2007, http://www.ithaka.org/strategic-services/university-publishing/ (accessed July 27, 2007), and Brown, Laura, Griffiths, Rebecca, and Rascoff, Matthew, "University Publishing in a Digital Age: Highlights of the Ithaka Report," *ARL: A Bimonthly Report on Research Library Issues and Actions from ARL, CNI, and SPARC* 252/253 (June/August 2007): 2–6.

4. Shulenburger, David, "University Research Publishing or Distribution Strategies?" *ARL: A Bimonthly Report on Research Library Issues and Actions from ARL, CNI, and SPARC* 252/253 (June/August 2007): 6–9.

5. Choudhury, G. Sayeed, "The Virtual Observatory Meets the Library," *The Journal of Electronic Publishing* 11:1 (Winter 2008). http://hdl.handle.net/2027/spo.3336451.0011.111 (accessed February 15, 2008).

6. Ibid.

7. Ibid., emphasis original.

8. Ibid.

9. Ibid.

10. Ma, Jin, *Metadata, SPEC Kit 298* (Washington, DC: Association of Research Libraries, July 2007), 52–53.

11. Cornell University Library, Digital Consulting & Production Services, http://dcaps.library.cornell.edu/ (accessed February 2, 2008).

12. Cornell University, Library Technical Services, Metadata Services, http://metadata.library.cornell.edu/services.html (accessed February 2, 2008).

13. Brown University Library, Center for Digital Initiatives, http://dl.lib.brown.edu/index.html (accessed February 2, 2008).

14. Ma, Jin, *Metadata*, 15.

15. Andy Guess, "Harvard Opts In to Opt-Out Plan," *Inside Higher Ed* (February 13, 2008), http://www.insidehighered.com/news/2008/02/13/openaccess (accessed February 13, 2008).

16. Harvard University, Faculty of Arts And Sciences, Agenda, Regular Meeting, Tuesday, February 12, 2008, http://www.fas.harvard.edu/~secfas/February_2008_Agenda.pdf (accessed February 17, 2008).

17. University of Houston Libraries, Institutional Repository Task Force, *Institutional Repositories, SPEC Kit 292* (Washington, DC: Association of Research Libraries, July 2006), 21.

18. Markey, Karen et al., *Census of Institutional Repositories in the United States: MIRACLE Project Research Findings* (Washington, DC: Council on Library and Information Resources, 2007), http://www.clir.org/pubs/reports/pub140/pub140.pdf (accessed January 28, 2008).

19. Ibid., Table 2.8, 18.

20. Ibid., Figure 8.2, 72.
21. University of Houston Libraries, *Institutional Repositories*, 19.
22. Markey, *Census of Institutional Repositories*, 57.
23. Mitchell, Robert, "Harvard to Collect, Disseminate Scholarly Articles for Faculty; Legislation Designed to Allow Greater Worldwide Access," *Harvard University Gazette Online*, February 13, 2008, http://www.news.harvard.edu/gazette/2008/02.14/99-fasvote.html (accessed March 1, 2008).
24. Ibid.
25. University of Houston Libraries, *Institutional Repositories*, 14.
26. Markey, *Census of Institutional Repositories*, 61.
27. U.S. Department of Health and Human Services, National Institutes of Health, National Institutes of Health Public Access, http://publicaccess.nih.gov/ (accessed March 1, 2008).
28. Association of Research Libraries (ARL), *Agenda for Developing E-Science in Research Libraries* (Washington, DC: Association of Research Libraries, November 2007), http://www.arl.org/bm~doc/ARL_Escience_final.pdf (accessed January 4, 2008).
29. Ibid., 13.
30. Ibid., 14.
31. Ibid., 13.
32. The University of Michigan and the University of Wisconsin each have separate mass digitization agreements with Google. The remaining CIC libraries have a single joint agreement with Google. Content from all of the projects as indicated in the agreements will be archived through a CIC-managed shared digital repository system.
33. Arms, William Y., "Cyberscholarship: High Performance Computing Meets Digital Libraries," *The Journal of Electronic Publishing* 11, no. 1 (Winter 2008), http://hdl.handle.net/2027/spo.3336451.0011.103 (accessed February 15, 2008).
34. Larsen, Ronald L., "On the Threshold of Cyberscholarship," *The Journal of Electronic Publishing* 11, no. 1 (Winter 2008), http://hdl.handle.net/2027/spo.3336451.0011.102 (accessed February 15, 2008). In this article Larsen reports on the findings of a joint NSF/JISC workshop on data-driven science and scholarship. He states: "It may well be the case that the emerging and potentially more compelling requirements for cyberscholarship will be better served by *superdata* centers that leverage economies of scale in both technology and operational efficiency than by a multitude of independent institutional repositories."
35. Hahn, Karla, e-mail message to author, January 28, 2008.
36. Penn State Romance Studies, Supporting Scholarship, Quality, and Access, 2007, http://dpubs.libraries.psu.edu/publication/psu.rs/about.html (accessed March 2, 2008).
37. Unsworth, John , "The Crisis in Scholarly Publishing in the Humanities," *ARL Bimonthly Report* 228 (June 2003), http://www.arl.org/bm~doc/crisis.pdf (accessed March 2, 2008).
38. IATH, Institute for Advanced Technology in the Humanities, http://www.iath.virginia.edu/ (accessed March 3, 2008).
39. The Walt Whitman Archive, ed. Ed Folsom and Kenneth M. Price, http://www.whitmanarchive.org/ (accessed March 5, 2008).

40. Gutenberg<e>, http://www.gutenberg-e.org/index.html (accessed March 3, 2008).

41. California Digital Library, eScholarship Publishing Program, http://www.cdlib.org/programs/escholarship.html (accessed March 3, 2008).

42. Public Knowledge Project, Open Journal Systems, http://pkp.sfu.ca/?q=ojs (accessed March 15, 2008). Articles about the University of Illinois at Chicago implementation of OJS can be found at: Case Mary M. and John Nancy R., "Opening Up Scholarly Information at the University of Illinois at Chicago," *First Monday* 12, no. 10 (2007), http://www.uic.edu/htbin/cgiwrap/bin/ojs/index.php/fm/article/viewArtiocle/1956/1833 (accessed November 10, 2007); and Mary, Case M. and John, Nancy R., "Publishing Journals@UIC," *ARL: A Bimonthly Report on Research Library Issues and Actions from ARL, CNI, and SPARC* 252/253 (June/August 2007): 12–15.

43. Choudhury, "Virtual Observatory."

44. EPIC, A New Organization and a New Strategic Plan, http://www.epic.columbia.edu/ (accessed March 4, 2008).

45. Candee, Catherine H., "The University of California as Publisher," *ARL: A Bimonthly Report on Research Library Issues and Actions from ARL, CNI, and SPARC* 252/253 (June/August 2007): 11, http://www.arl.org/bm˜doc/arl-br-252–253-cal.pdf (accessed March 4, 2008).

# Reinventing Our Work: New and Emerging Roles for Academic Librarians

Lori A. Goetsch

**ABSTRACT.** Technology, globalization, and increasing competition for students, faculty, and research dollars have significantly affected the teaching and research efforts on our campuses. In response to meeting new and emerging user needs, libraries are crafting new roles and responsibilities for librarians by both reinventing more traditional positions as well as creating new job roles that require skill sets that, at present, are not learned through library and information science education and training. This paper will examine the impacts, benefits, and tensions that this changing workforce has on academic libraries, with a particular focus on a content analysis of selected job vacancy announcements in the last decade.

## *SUMMARY*

Technology has significantly influenced how students and faculty use the services and collections of academic libraries. In response, libraries are identifying new roles and responsibilities for librarians by both reinventing more traditional positions as well as creating new job roles that require different skill sets and mind sets. This paper will examine the impacts, benefits, and tensions this changing workforce has on academic libraries by

---

Lori A. Goetsch is Dean of Libraries, Kansas State University, 504 Hale Library, Manhattan, KS.

analyzing position vacancy announcements and speculating on librarians' roles in the future.

## INTRODUCTION

Those of you of a certain age can recall what kind of work you were doing professionally twenty-five years ago or so. As a reference librarian, I was serving on a desk about twenty hours per week, working from a print reference collection and a first-generation automated circulation system. I taught bibliographic instruction sessions using an overhead projector to show students sample pages from the *Readers Guide to Periodical Literature* and the library's green-bar serials holdings list. My exposure to computers and automation in library school was an assignment using an OCLC "beehive" terminal and another using punch cards and a knitting needle. I also conducted one online search in DIALOG to fulfill a course requirement. When I am asked today about the changes in our profession, I find myself exclaiming that I could not have envisioned that we would be working the way we are today. Our services, collections, facilities—everything! —have been dramatically transformed.

Fifteen years into my career, I presented a paper at the Association of College and Research Libraries (ACRL) conference in Nashville entitled "Libraries and the Post-Job Organization."[1] It was prompted by a William Bridges article published in *Fortune* called "The End of the Job,"[2] based on his book *JobShift*.[3] I was drawn to his work because of what I was seeing in my own job as a head of reference—a department furiously adapting to the emergence of the Internet and other technological advances. We were shifting from print to electronic resources and from mediated online searching to end user searching in what seemed like a blink of an eye. We were anxious about our future. Once the users got their hands on those resources directly, what would our jobs be? What would we do when we were no longer the authority or at least the mediator? Bridges's work helped me to put these changes in a larger perspective, that of the postjob organization. While the postjob organization has several characteristics, the most notable to me at the time, and today, is that the work is defined by customer needs and not a job description. What that meant in 1997 was that the customers were getting information on computers in the library and soon, we knew, on their office and home desktops. What would our users need that would guide our new work?

Ten years later, in reflecting back on that paper and on our profession, library work and organizations have been increasingly confronted with the challenges and opportunities of technology among many other forces. How are we responding in the first decade of the twenty-first century? Are we creating library jobs that address new and emerging user needs? What are the skills sets needed to do this work? This paper will consider the impacts, benefits, and tensions that this changing workforce has on academic libraries since 1995 through the lens of specific library positions—systems librarians, reference librarians, and subject librarians—and some speculation about how the changes in these positions over the past decade or so serve as predictors for the future.

These jobs were selected because their responsibilities have changed and overlapped as a result of a rapidly evolving technological environment. For example, systems librarians moved from working in a mainframe to a client-server environment, and users of their services migrated from stand-alone computers to networked workstations to handheld devices over that same period. In many libraries, these changes have pushed systems and information technology librarians out of the server room and into public spaces and interactions, such as usability testing. In turn, reference librarians had to master the transition from print to electronic resources. They have gone from mediating those resources on behalf of the user through online search services to helping the user on site and remotely with a vast amount of electronic information that is provided by a number of different sources of which the library is only one. As a result, reference librarians have had to become increasingly technologically literate, incorporating some of the skill sets of a systems or information technology librarian, as information and productivity tools have converged on the desktop. The subject librarian is a well-established position, an outgrowth of the bibliographer of earlier days, and has expanded to include the reference, instruction, and liaison responsibilities. These roles come together in the subject librarian based on both a philosophical and practical view that each responsibility informs the other. Similar to reference librarians, subject librarians have had to adapt to technological change in their reference and instruction work as well as in how they fulfill their collection development responsibilities. Rather than focusing on print collections, selection of electronic resources now dominates the collection development landscape and an increasing number of nontraditional sources of information are emerging.

## *LITERATURE REVIEW*

Several content analyses of position descriptions have appeared in the literature. In 1997, Dolan and Schumacher discussed both redefined and new jobs, noting that new positions are emerging in special libraries while academic libraries "often just redefine existing jobs."[4] They go on to note, however, that "lately, a refreshing trend has been seen in job advertisements from academic institutions requiring state-of-the-art technical skills."[5] Those skills include "networking concepts and configurations, modern-day programming (with C++, Java, or CGI scripts), HTML literacy, advanced operating system skills, and more."[6] In addition, the authors note that, "these skills must be combined with the specialized expertise of library training and wedded with interpersonal/ communication skills and subject knowledge."[7] Dolan and Schumacher also observe that library schools are revamping curricula to catch up with these new skills sets.

Five years later, Croneis and Henderson analyzed job announcements with the term "electronic" or "digital" in the title, noting the differences based on size of library as well as the great variety of titles used to describe new work across an organization in both public and technical services areas.[8] Fisher reports on a study of the position of electronic resources librarian and notes that in more cases than he expected, public service skills were a fundamental part of the position announcement.[9] In 2003, *Library Hi Tech* published a special issue on systems librarians and their changing roles, responsibilities, and placement in the library organization. Articles include a discussion on the status of systems librarians within academic libraries over time, an examination of how the position has evolved in a single library, and the diversification of work as technology becomes more ubiquitous and end user accessible.[10] Choi and Rasmussen's 2006 study of activities and skills of "digital librarians" notes that "about 40 percent of the respondents had been involved in digital library work from other functional areas" including collection development and management.[11]

Other content analyses of position announcements include Beile and Adams, which focused on ads appearing in 1996; a comprehensive study by Lynch and Smith published in 2001 that analyzes *College and Research Libraries News* advertisements from 1973 to 1998; and Kennan, Willard, and Wilson's 2006 analysis of position vacancies in Australian libraries across three decades.[12] All document the trend towards requiring computer skills, with the latter article noting changes in terminology from automation to digital or electronic skills. As with the Dolan and Schumacher study, these authors also note the parallel rise of requirements for interpersonal skills.

There is also literature that focuses specifically on the subject librarian. White reports results of a content analysis of subject specialist positions in business, social sciences, and science from 1990 to 1998. In addition to an excellent review of the literature on position announcement analyses prior to his research, his article is a good snapshot of the job market and requirements for subject librarians during most of the nineties. Among the findings from his study, White notes the "steady growth in the percentage of announcements listing electronic resources as a job responsibility" and that "computer skills also ranked high and were the second most frequently cited skill for science, and the fourth for business and social sciences."[13] He concludes, "Computer technology is a skill often listed as 'desired' or 'preferred.' Internet or Web skills are also relatively highly placed, especially when considering that these skills were not necessary in the early part of the decade."[14] In a 2001 article about the status of subject librarians in the United Kingdom, Stephen Pinfield discusses the changing role of the subject librarian as "the old job...plus," the plus being new or differently emphasized roles and the skills sets required—e-resources selection and management, educational technology applications and new learning environments, and effective communications and interpersonal skills for liaison work.[15]

## SELECTED JOB ANNOUNCEMENTS: 1995, 2000, AND 2005

To develop my own understanding of the impact of technology and other changes on the roles and responsibilities of these job positions in academic libraries, I selected three years—1995, 2000, and 2005—and examined ads in *College and Research Libraries News (C & RL News)*. The time span was selected to coincide with some landmark technological events and advancements and is a snapshot of an era of rapid change in libraries' and society's use of technology. As context, it is helpful to briefly capture some of these key technology events. The Netscape browser and the first search engines debuted in 1994, and by 1995, Netscape went public on the stock exchange. The Palm Pilot was introduced in 1996, Internet Explorer debuted in1997, SPARC was formed in 1997–98, and Google was developed and unveiled between 1998–99. Between 2000 and 2005, the iPOD was introduced (2001), Google Print was launched (2004–5), and YouTube arrived on the scene (2005).[16] Each by itself has had a significant impact on our work; combined together, they are a nearly mind-boggling array of new technologies in a short period of time.

The primary purpose of this analysis is to look at job titles, responsibilities, and requirements, with the positions being broadly defined. Subject librarian positions had to have, first and foremost, an obvious subject focus and, second, generally include responsibility for reference services, collection development, and library instruction. Systems librarian positions were selected solely on the use of that title as well as a few related titles that emerged during the study. For reference librarians, I focused on positions reflecting technological impact on the title, for example, electronic resources or electronic reference librarian. Management and administrative positions were excluded as were bibliographer positions that focused strictly on collection development and management.

In 1995, *C & RL News* position vacancy announcements were chock full of "electronically"-enhanced job titles, sending the message that skills, experience, and interest in working with technology in a rapidly changing environment was essential to successful job candidates. Job titles in reference services are most evident in terms of incorporated technology language—for example, Electronic Services Librarian, Electronic Reference Librarian, Reference/Database Access Librarian, and Reference Librarian for Networked Resources. Responsibilities and requirements for these positions include online searching, teaching end user searching, familiarity with print and electronic reference sources, and microcomputer applications in reference services including knowledge of software packages and operating systems. Specific systems and tools are mentioned in many cases: CDRom networks, LANs, Mosaic (in one case), and DIALOG, for example.

At the same time, many institutions posted positions for Systems Librarians. In a handful of institutions, Information Technology Librarian is used as an alternative job title and, in one case, Electronic Resources Librarian, a title that resurfaces with different expectations in the coming years, was used. Responsibilities and requirements include working with operating systems, databases, software, and telecommunications and management of networks and the integrated library system. Less frequently—in fact, in only two ads—Gopher and Web server administration is mentioned and, in one ad, homepage creation. In some cases, familiarity with specific integrated library systems and programming languages is required or preferred.

When it comes to subject librarians, many of the technology-based requirements for the electronic reference positions are also expected to a greater or lesser degree. All announcements asked for knowledge or experience related to technology, although the way the skills are framed varies widely and includes microcomputer skills, database searching, online searching, computer applications, and computer-based tools. Six ads specifically mention the Internet, two the World Wide Web/Gopher, and only one institution uses the word "digital" in its announcement.

While online mediated searching experience is still required or desirable, knowledge and ability to work with end user searching is beginning to appear. Other skills required are common to a more traditional subject librarian role including a second advanced degree, foreign language knowledge, and subject knowledge or experience required or preferred.

By 2000, Google had saturated our world and the "E" word has nearly disappeared from general reference librarian titles. The Electronic Resources or Electronic Services Librarian title has emerged to describe a more specialized role, typically that of the lead person in a reference or collection development department who is responsible for all manner of electronic resource vendor selection, access, licensing, and use. Skills and knowledge requirements include print and electronic resource options and vendors, Web applications and development, software and hardware management, staff training, and usage statistics. Candidates must meet a higher level of technical skills and experience than other reference positions. In essence, this person interfaces between technology and content on behalf of the reference or subject librarian. These hybrid positions occasionally reside in the library's systems department but are often still expected to provide reference services and instruction as part of their duties.

Web addresses are also appearing in ads by this time, and the promise of the Web as a tool for delivering instruction and information has emerged. Job titles that reflect this change include Web Services Librarian, Web Development Librarian, and Library Web Manager. "Digital" has also become part of the job title: Digital Services Librarian, Digital Support Librarian, Digital Collections Librarian, Digital Initiatives Librarian, Digital Projects Librarian, and Digital Resources Librarian. In some cases, these positions report to the systems department or division of the organization. A few positions report to public services where responsibilities include reference service along with Web page creation and management. Requirements for skills and experience include Windows NT, Web publishing, and desktop computing. Some very specialized positions are being advertised that reflect the emerging digital library as well as technology-enhanced instruction, e.g., Interface Specialist, Instructional Design Librarian, Media Development Librarian, and Electronic Text and Imaging Librarian. Systems librarians, by that and other titles, are still being sought, and responsibility for the integrated library system and the Web is common. In several cases, responsibilities and requirements often overlap with other functional areas in either public or technical services.

Subject librarian announcements reflect these trends as well. The development and maintenance of Web pages is a key qualification in most ads for subject librarians. Other skills being sought by employers included database development, image digitization and management, and experience with consortial efforts for developing electronic resources and digital collections. Positions in the humanities state a preferred requirement of knowledge or experience with electronic texts. The impact of technology on scholarly communications in various disciplines is creeping into some ads as is user needs assessment, but not extensively. Other technology-related skills as outlined from the 1995 announcements are now commonplace in ads and geared towards the end user. Again, the more traditional requirements remain and instruction is also increasingly emphasized in comparison to 1995.

By 2005, Systems Librarians have almost disappeared from the job listings, either because titles have changed to reflect new roles and responsibilities or because these positions are being advertised elsewhere. Announcements appear for specialized positions such as Digital Applications and Systems Librarian, Digital Initiatives Librarian, Web Development Librarian, Interface and User Testing Specialist, Library System Developer, and Web Services Librarian. Also nearly gone is telegraphing the technology aspects of a position in the job title for reference positions. A few titles still use the term "electronic" such as Electronic and Instructional Services Librarian, Electronic Resources Librarian, and Electronic Services Librarian. An interesting change, however, is that there are positions where Electronic Resources Librarian is now used to describe a librarian working in the technical services side of the house on licensing and cataloging e-resources rather than in reference or collection development.

For subject librarians, most requirements remain constant, however, information literacy appears even more strongly as a requirement with specific references to the *Information Literacy Competency Standards for Higher Education*,[17] development of Web applications for learning, interfacing with course management systems, and online learning communities appearing in many job announcements. In several ads, instruction predominates over reference or collection development in job responsibilities and skill requirements. Librarian as research partner is also evident in 2005 announcements from Purdue and MIT. The MIT ad includes the language, "monitor research development in the departments and labs to identify and foster potential applications or research partnerships in support of the operations and research agenda of the MIT Libraries."[18]

## *FINDINGS AND OBSERVATIONS*

We have quickly transitioned from viewing technology-related skills as special or unique to considering them essential. This is evident in how job announcements describe the skills needed, the relative emphasis given to these skills in job ads, and how positions are titled. The move away from placing the word "electronic" in front of a number of traditional job titles is just one indication of that shift. Another is that certain job requirements and titles have moved around through the typical organizational units of an academic library. The use of the title Electronic Resources Librarian to represent a public services position, then a systems position, and subsequently a technical services position is a good example. This wandering job title may also suggest that what we mean by public services, technical services, collection development, systems, and other terms we have used to define our organizational structure is breaking apart and changing as these boundaries blur.

In addition to the shifts from print to electronic resources and stand-alone to networked computing reflected in the vacancy announcements, other tipping points have played an important part in changing job responsibilities and requirements. Many relate to how we develop library collections. We own less of our newly acquired information resources and license more, so as that licensing work has become more common, if not routine, it has migrated to production units such as technical services. Content bundled in manageable and describable packets, like the journal issue, is "unbundling." The open access movement; institutional repositories; the rise of new forms of sharing and communicating information such as blogs, wikis, and their successors; and locally created digital libraries challenge us to think differently about what our collections are and what our users' needs are for those collections and, therefore, how we describe the skills needed to build those collections.

In a 2007 *First Monday* article, Heather Morrison provides an excellent example of this shift from her own experience as a librarian, an author, and a user. She writes, "If libraries focus solely on collecting peer-reviewed or formally published literature and not blogs and listservs, some of my best writings, and some of the ideas contained there and not expressed elsewhere, are likely to be lost." Morrison goes on to say that "the discrete 'item'—the book, the journal article—is becoming less relevant in today's interconnected world. The collection of the future may be a collection of collections of interrelated and/or interlinked items." These items of the future include full text works, preprints, grants, lab notes, blogs, conference Web casts, repositories, data, and other means of communication that we do not even know about yet.[19]

As collections are rethought, so are the services and systems that support those collections. Google has taken center stage in the provision of information to the end user including the information purchased by and provided through the library. Consequently, reference and subject librarians are employing a variety of applications to reach out and offer virtual assistance to users—e-mail, chat, instant messaging, and whatever comes next—while traffic at our reference desks declines. At the same time, the integrated library system that has been supported by systems librarians and has served as the foundation for the acquisition, organization, and access to our collections is disintegrating as new options, including open source solutions and reference linking software, appear on the marketplace. The development and implementation of these new systems will redefine the library catalog and require a different kind of integration, the integration of a skill set that incorporates an understanding of user needs and customer service, information organization and access in a disintegrated environment, and new and emerging modes of communicating information and research.

## *THE POSTJOB LIBRARY REDUX*

In a recent editorial in *Journal of Academic Librarianship*, Rush Miller writes, "With our 'legacy' collections moving into storage and our buildings being retrofitted for more emphasis on teaching and learning, group activities, coffee shops, etc., fundamental library change is already well underway."[20] The evolution of academic librarian roles and responsibilities in the past decade suggest that, to recall William Bridges' work, we are behaving like postjob organizations. We are changing to meet user needs, often in a reactionary mode, but changing nonetheless. We have recognized the importance of assessment and marketing, and we are rethinking our professional education and retooling and retraining our staff. There are other signs of our efforts to become more responsive and anticipatory of changes ahead, from ACRL's "Top Ten Assumptions for the Future of Libraries and Librarians"[21] and the Taiga Forum's 2006 "Provocative Statements"[22] to the 21st Century Librarian grants funded by the Institute for Museum and Library Services. Certainly, we are in a transformative time in our profession, and, as Miller's quote suggests, we are eager to remain relevant on our campus.

The next evolution of library positions will play a key role in that effort to remain relevant, and the trends of the past decade help to paint a picture of possible futures for librarians. By drawing on the core roles and responsibilities of positions such as systems librarians (high-level technological expertise), reference librarians (user assistance and education), and subject librarians (collection development and management and liaison work), a re-envisioned and interrelated set of four new core responsibilities emerges: consulting services; information lifecycle management; collaborative print and electronic collection building; and information mediation and interpretation.

Consulting services expand on subject librarian responsibilities and the model of resident or "embedded" subject librarians popular in the late 1990s and build on the idea of librarian as research partner reflected in the MIT ad referenced earlier. They incorporate the core work of collection development, reference, and instruction with expanded liaison responsibilities for repository services, e.g., working with faculty and graduate students on copyright, author rights, and intellectual property issues; alternative publishing outlets for research and scholarship including locally support platforms for publishing; and depositing and managing faculty and student scholarship in local or other repositories. This role is already in place in several libraries as a scholarly communications librarian or other similar title. However, as repositories grow, new publishing models catch fire, and public policy initiatives like the National Institutes of Health open access policy spread to other funding agencies, it is likely that a tipping point will occur that will push these responsibilities into core duties for several librarians in an organization, not just one or two. Subject librarians are already well-positioned for this work because of their in-depth interactions on a disciplinary level with faculty and students.

Another emerging core responsibility that could very well be incorporated into the role of the librarians providing the consulting services discussed above is the information lifecycle management—the curation of research, institutional and cultural records, both physical and digital, and the creation and maintenance of repositories. Traditionally the purview at least in part of the archivist, this new skill set will be needed to respond to the growing number of electronic institutional records, from administrative documents to online curriculum and more, as well as the research output of the university. The work combines archival sciences and electronic records management with subject expertise and collection management and development skills. Positions that integrate these skills sets will be needed to solve the challenges created by technology such as how we capture born digital items and how we work with administrators and faculty at the point of document creation so that the resulting product and its related elements, such as data, can be retained, accessed, and preserved for future generations.

A third core responsibility redefines collection selection responsibilities from building a local collection that is loaned globally through interlibrary loan to developing collaborative, shared print collections. Shared collections will be built based on cooperative agreements with partner institutions or consortia that will, in essence, carve up the print world for acquisition and storage, not unlike the shared regional federal depository models already in place or under development. Rapid document delivery, interlibrary loan, cooperative storage facilities, and e-books as well as changes in print publishing and repurposing library acquisitions funds will all conspire to create a tipping point that will move us from measuring libraries by the size of their collections to maximizing our resources and reallocating those resources to meet user needs. In turn, shared general collections will open up the opportunity, time, and, perhaps, funds to rethink how special collections are defined and built. The selection of rare books and manuscripts will no longer be strictly the purview of special collections librarians but will become the focal point of our local collection building efforts. Furthermore, these unique collections will not just be acquired for our user communities but will be the foundation for digital initiatives as we make those collections available globally.

The fourth core responsibility for librarians—information mediation and interpretation—is best articulated in Susan Gibbons's recent book about the University of Rochester library experience, *The Academic Library and the Net Gen Student: Making the Connections.* Gibbons writes, "Academic librarians, particularly subject specialists, are important as both disciplinary insiders and outsiders. . . . The importance of this dual role . . . can be critical in the successful transmission of knowledge between professor and student. . . . The librarian can act as a translator between the apprentices (students) and discipline masters (professors)."[23] Gibbons draws on Web 2.0 capabilities as the bridge between students and professors that librarians can help each group cross. She advises librarians to develop a research and development culture; rethink the meaning of place; encourage digital authorship by modeling use of blogs, wikis, and social networking tools; and be active learners about our users.

It seems quite possible that these four emerging and overlapping responsibilities could find their way into a single position, a new renaissance librarian that brings together the skill sets of a subject librarian, an archivist or records manager, a reference and instruction librarian, and a systems or information technology librarian. Surrounding this new generalist and providing the infrastructure that supports them are functional layers that reflect, in many respects, Bridges' postjob organization, e.g., assessment, marketing, information systems coordination, research and development, and facilities planning and utilization. There are many implications for the emergence of the new renaissance librarian, three key implications being the future of library and information science education, the need for skill sets that sit outside of library and information science, and workload management. Interwoven throughout is the need to question our assumptions about our work and our behaviors toward that work.

As initiatives like the IMLS 21st Century Librarian and education forums at ALA conferences suggest, we are already actively rethinking our educational requirements. Newly minted librarians are engaging in this dialog and offering a critical perspective and an important voice on the future of the MLS. An excellent example is the blog, Information Wants to be Free, authored by Meredith Farkas. In a 2006 posting, Farkas began a discussion and list of basic to high level competencies for the twenty-first century librarian. One of the more interesting aspects of her post is that Farkas focuses her competencies not just on technological and related skills such as assessment and project management but on behavior and attitude. Examples include the ability to embrace change, comfort in an online medium, and enthusiasm for learning, all postjob qualities. Over forty responses build on the competency list and comment—sometimes quite vehemently—on the state of library education. As a snapshot in time, the Farkas posting is representative of discussions going on across the profession about our future and whether or not we even have one as well as what kinds of skills, hard and soft, we are going to need to be successful.

Another implication is that there are skills sets, and professionals who have those skill sets, which libraries will need to provide foundational or infrastructure support to the new work. Some of these skills may be developed from within an organization through training; others will come from outside the profession. For example, Gibbons's book is based on work conducted with a resident anthropologist. Also, academic libraries are acting on the need for grant writers, fundraisers, marketing and public relations specialists, graphic artists, numerical and spatial data specialists, electronic records managers, copyright and intellectual property experts, and instructional designers in growing numbers. Adding these skills sets to the mix will test our thinking about credentials, recruitment, retention, and professional status. The "soft skills" that Bridges references and Farkas promotes—flexibility, continuous learning, comfort with ambiguity, and the ability to retool and retrain—will become even more critical in this changing organizational environment.

The third implication harkens back to Pinfield's lament that this new work sounds like the "old job plus." We must confront and question how we can rethink workflows, services, and other efforts in order to take work out of the system that is not meeting the needs of our users. This has been a struggle throughout my professional life and is not likely to be easily resolved but must be attempted, even incrementally. The ACRLog's recent postings on obsolete academic librarian skills have been an entertaining if not educational look at work that has, in fact, disappeared from librarian's jobs, from typing and filing cataloging cards and lining up tractor-feed paper to policing food and drink and dozens more. All seem small and almost laughable until added together and put in the context of the larger changes happening around them such as the disappearance of the card catalog and multiple new ways to capture and output information rather than printing. Are we able to look now at the day-to-day work and find other tasks and workflows that could be eliminated or reengineered? One modest suggestion is that we should be de-emphasizing the title by title selection and acquisitions of print material. By replacing that process with comprehensive approval or purchase plans, either locally or in concert with other libraries as described above, materials can go from the loading dock to the shelf with little intervention. This tipping point will enable librarians to repurpose their time and skills to the new work.

## *CONCLUSION*

This brave new library sounds suspiciously like what I walked into over twenty-five years ago when I was told the importance of having a high tolerance for ambiguity, being creative with limited resources, and adapting quickly to change. We do now what we did then—acknowledge that the world of information and the world of technology are not what they were in the previous decade. Nevertheless, our adaptability, as reflected in the evolution of job responsibilities and requirements in the past decade, as well as our sound professional values and foundational tenets may hold us in good stead in the new century. As Gibbons notes, "The Internet and Web cannot replace the academic library because, although technology can be a better information provider, it cannot substitute for the essential role of humans in the creation, transmission, and dissemination of knowledge."[24] And we are not alone in the information professions in facing this change. Richard Pearce-Moses, in his presidential address to the Society of American Archivists in 2007, echoes the argument that what we do will not change as much as how we do it. In his address entitled "Janus in Cyberspace: Archives on the Threshold of the Digital Era," Moses elaborates on the theme that we have one face looking back and another looking forward, leaving one place while entering another. He writes, "We need more than knowledge and skills to thrive in the digital world. We need new attitudes. A new frontier lies on the other side of the digital doorway, and it's not for the faint of heart."[25]

## NOTES

1. Goetsch, Lori A., "Libraries and the Post-Job Organization," http://www.ala.org/ala/acrlbucket/nashville1997pap/goetsch.cfm.

2. Bridges William, "The End of the Job," *Fortune* (September 19, 1994): 62–74.

3. Bridges, *JobShift* (Reading, MA: Addison-Wesley, 1994).

4. Dolan, Donna R., and Schumacher, John, "New Jobs Emerging in and around Libraries and Librarianship," *Online* 21 (November/December 1997): 68.

5. Ibid.

6. Ibid.

7. Ibid.

8. Croneis, Karen S., and Henderson, Pat, "Electronic and Digital Librarian Positions: A Content Analysis of Announcements form 1990 through 2000," *Journal of Academic Librarianship* 28, no. 4 (July/August 2002): 232–237.

9. Fisher William, "The Electronic Resources Librarian Position: A Public Services Phenomenon?" *Library Collections, Acquisitions, & Technical Services* 27 (2003): 3–17.

10. *Library Hi Tech* 21, no. 3 (2003).

11. Choi, Youngok, and Rasmussen, Edie, "What Is Needed to Educate Future Digital Libraries: A Study of Current Practice and Staffing Patterns in Academic and Research Libraries," *D-Lib Magazine* 12, no. 9 (September 2006): 1.

12. Beile, Penny M., and Adams, Megan M., "Other Duties as Assigned: Emerging Trends in the Academic Library Job Market," *College and Research Libraries* 61, no. 4 (July 2000): 336–347; Lynch, Beverly P., and Smith, Kimberley Robles, "The Changing Nature of Work in Academic Libraries," *College and Research Libraries* 62, no. 5 (2001): 407–420; Kennan, Mary Anne, Willard, Patricia, and Wilson, Concepcion S.,

"What Do They Want?: A Study of Changing Employer Expectations of Information Professionals," *Australian Academic and Research Libraries* 37, no. 1 (March 2006): 17–37.

13. White, Gary W., "Academic Subject Specialist Positions in the United States: A Content Analysis of Announcements from 1990 through 1998," *Journal of Academic Librarianship* 25, no. 5 (1999): 372–382.

14. Ibid.

15. Pinfield, Stephen, "The Changing Role of Subject Librarians in Academic Libraries," *Journal of Librarianship and Information Science* 33, no. 1 (March 2001): 34.

16. For examples of technology timelines, see http://www.isrl.uiuc.edu/~chip/projects/timeline/; http://www.librarytechnology.org/automationhistory.pl; and http://www/zakon/org/robert/internet/timeline/.

17. *Information Literacy Competency Standards in Higher Education*, http://www.ala.org/ala/acrl/acrlstandards/informationliteracycompetency.cfm.

18. *College & Research Libraries News* 66, no. 6 (June 2005): 496.

19. Morrison, Heather, "Rethinking Collections—Libraries and Librarians in the Open Age: A Theoretical View," *First Monday* 12, no. 10 (October 1, 2007), http://www.uic.edu/htbin/cgiwrap/bin/ojs/index.php/fm/issue/view/250.

20. Miller, Rush, "What Difference Do We Make?" *Journal of Academic Librarianship* 33, no. 1 (January 2007): 1–2.

21. Mullins, James L., Allen, Frank R., and Hufford Jon R., "Top Ten Assumptions for the Future of Academic Libraries and Librarians: A Report from the ACRL Research Committee," *College & Research Libraries News* 68, no. 4 (April 2007): 240–246.

22. Taiga Forum Steering Committee, Taiga Forum Provocative Statements, March 10, 2006, http://www.taigaforum.org/documents/ProvocativeStatements.pdf.

23. Gibbons, Susan, *The Academic Library and the Net Gen Student: Making the Connections* (Chicago: American Library Association, 2007), 9.

24. Ibid., 11.

25. Moses, Richard Pearce, "Janus in Cyberspace: Archives on the Threshold of the Digital Era," *The American Archivist* 70 (Spring/Summer 2007): 13–22.

# Attitudes and Behaviors in the Field of Economics: Anomaly or Leading Indicator

Kevin Guthrie
Ross Housewright

**ABSTRACT.** This paper will explore the challenges and opportunities that libraries face in the digital world from the perspective of a single disciplinary field: economics. Through analysis of faculty surveys, interviews with economists, and assessment of the impact of new digital resources and services that have emerged to support the field, we will highlight how the behaviors and attitudes of this field have changed in a very short period of time. What kind of services do the economists need from libraries, and perhaps more importantly, from librarians? Are the changes in behavior of economists over the last decade, which have been characterized by a dramatic reduction in their dependence on the traditional library, anomalous and specific to the field, or are they predictive of broader trends? What might this mean for the choices that librarians must make in order to support scholarship?

## *INTRODUCTION*

On the day that a scholar used the same search resource to find an important article in their field of study as they used to find the nearest place

---

Kevin Guthrie is President, Ithaka, New York, NY (E-mail: kevin.guthrie@ithaka.org).

Ross Housewright is Research Analyst, Ithaka, New York, NY (E-mail: ross.housewright@ithaka.org).

to get a slice of pizza, the world of scholarship was forever altered. No longer was the world of scholarly inquiry and the academy insulated from the commercial world. The pace, scale, and relentless pursuit of progress in the commercial networked economy has flooded the academy.

It is said that a rising tide floats all boats. That is surely true, provided that the boats are sea worthy. This is a sea of networked technology and digital information. Since the scholarly community's core product is knowledge, and knowledge can now be transformed into bits and bytes, everything either has changed, is changing, or can change. Reflecting on it for a moment, it is not easy to think of parts of the academic enterprise that have not been impacted. Research habits. Information storage and retrieval. Teaching methods. The list goes on and on. There is no choice but to set out to sea, and as sailors like to say: There is weather.

There is nothing new in this metaphor; we have all read 100 articles about the need to change and the need for libraries to move along. But what to do, and how does one set priorities among a seemingly infinite array of possibilities? Sorry, we are not going to provide answers to such questions, but we are going to share some data, anecdotes, and reactions that we hope will provoke creative thinking within local library contexts that might stimulate steps to gather information and frame options in actionable ways. It is essential that libraries understand and use these kinds of data because libraries' success is threatened if they are not effectively serving the needs of important campus constituents, and serving those constituents is becoming competitive. This is no longer a captive audience; students and faculty can and are getting their research and information needs fulfilled in whole or in part from services offered outside the campus environment via the network. In a world of limited resources, being competitive requires that libraries be strategic.

## *ITHAKA'S RESEARCH*

Since 2000, we have been interested in how new technologies are impacting faculty attitudes and behaviors. First at JSTOR, and subsequently at Ithaka, we have commissioned an outside research firm, Odyssey, to conduct large-scale studies of faculty in order to learn more about their attitudes toward the transition to an increasingly electronic environment. We conducted these surveys in the fall of 2000, 2003, and 2006. In 2006, we supplemented the faculty research with a study of librarian attitudes and behaviors, asking many of the same questions of librarians that we had been asking of faculty. The most recent iteration of the faculty survey generated 4,100 responses and the librarian study, which targeted collection development directors, generated 350 responses. These studies were cosponsored by JSTOR and Ithaka's incubated entities Portico, Aluka, and NITLE. Our objective was to examine attitudes and perceptions related to scholarly communications, research practices, and classroom teaching.

This paper presents an overview of some of the data gathered in these studies, focusing on the question of how libraries can serve faculty needs in a rapidly changing environment. We will provide a general picture of how scholars in different disciplines perceive and use the library as well as a more detailed portrait of the field of economics, which has changed substantially in the last several years from a primarily paper-based to an almost exclusively digital discipline. One reason for sharing these data and results is to try to provide for librarians a sense of the trends in these behaviors as a way of helping identify possible ways for them to engage with, anticipate, and prepare for change. For example, one obvious conclusion to draw from the changes in the economists' attitudes and behaviors is that work patterns are not immutable but change based on the resources and tools available. As those patterns change with access to digital information and tools, the services needed by these users change as well. If one agrees with this proposition, one would then conclude that it is very important to actively engage in understanding the changing needs, motivations, incentives and behaviors of faculty so that one can aim library services at the present and future needs of this critical constituency.

## FACULTY MEMBER ATTITUDES TOWARD LIBRARIES

When data collected in 2006 are compared with findings from 2000 and 2003, it will be a surprise to no one that faculty increasingly value electronic resources. At the same time, while they value the library, they perceive themselves to be decreasingly dependent on the library for their research and teaching, and they anticipate that dependence to continue to decline in the future. There appears to be growing ambivalence about the campus library.

On the positive side, the vast majority of faculty view the role that librarians play as important as it has been in the past. This view is held relatively equally across different types of institutions, except among faculty at research universities, where it is somewhat less strongly supported (60 percent of faculty at research institutions said that the librarians' role was just as important as it was in the past, compared to 70 percent at all institutions).

These responses do however vary by discipline. Humanities faculty generally see the librarian's role as having greater continuing importance than do social scientists, who in turn are more optimistic than scientists. More than 80 percent of humanities faculty think that the librarian's role remains just as important, but less than 60 percent of scientists support that opinion—social scientists fall in the middle at around 70 percent (see Figure 1). This is representative of a general pattern—humanities scholars generally feel closer ties to libraries, presumably due to their greater research reliance on monographs, archives, and other material not yet widely available in digital formats, while scientists are the least reliant upon traditional library-provided search tools (see Figure 2).

Even within these broad disciplinary groupings, however, there may be substantial variation. While about 80 percent of sociology faculty feel that the role of librarians is of continuing importance on their campus, only about 30 percent of economists, also counted among social scientists, agreed with this view (see Figure 3). The individual characteristics of a particular discipline, the resources available to it in digital and analog form, and a number of other factors may influence a discipline's relationship with the library.

FIGURE 1. Percent of faculty agreeing strongly with the statement "Even though faculty have easy access to academic content online, the role librarians play at this institution is just as important as it has been in the past."

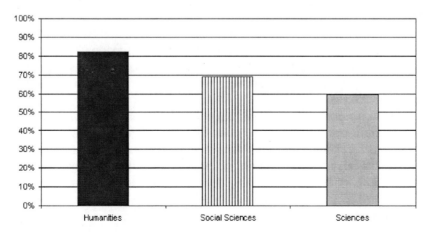

FIGURE 2. Faculty opinions on the statement "With the advent of digitized books and search tools that are widely available to all users over the Internet, traditional catalogs used by scholars and provided by my library (traditional catalogs, e-catalogs, journal indexing databases, and similar tools) are becoming irrelevant for faculty and students," by discipline.

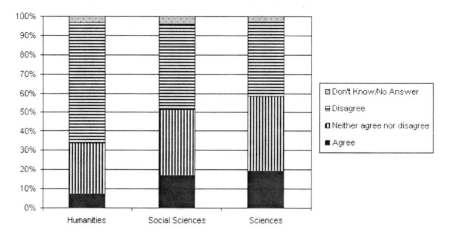

## *Changing Roles of the Library*

Over the course of these three surveys, we have tested three "roles" of the library–purchaser, archive, and gateway[1]– and we have attempted to track how the importance of these three different roles have changed over time. Most highly rated among these roles is that of library as purchaser. The faculty does not want to have to pay for scholarly resources. This is true across all disciplines. There is somewhat more variation by discipline in views on the importance of the library's preservation function, but valuation of this role is also uniformly high. The role of the library as a gateway for locating information, however, is dropping with each successive survey.

This is a concern in general, but it is even more of a concern when one focuses on specific disciplines. The importance of this role has decreased for faculty across all disciplines since 2003, most significantly among scientists. While almost 80 percent of humanists rate this role as very important, barely over 50 percent of scientists do similarly (see Figure 3). The decreasing importance of this role to faculty is logical given the increasing prominence of nonlibrary discovery tools such as

FIGURE 3. Percent of faculty rating these library roles as "very important," by discipline.

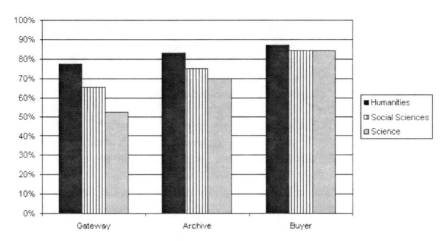

Google in the last several years. Since 2003, more scholars across disciplines report starting their research at nonlibrary discovery tools, either a general-purpose search engine or a specific electronic resource, and fewer report starting in directly library-related venues, either the library building or the library OPAC (see Figure 4).

FIGURE 4. Starting point for research identified by faculty, in 2003 and 2006

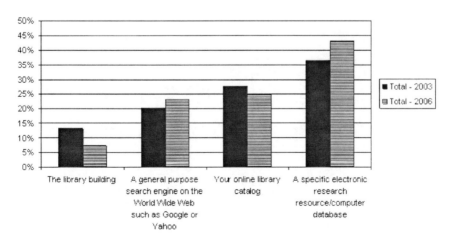

Here we bring in results from our 2006 librarian survey. Although faculty perception of the library as an important gateway is decreasing rather dramatically in certain fields, librarians list this gateway role as very important to faculty at a very high rate—over 90 percent (see Figure 5). Obviously, there is a mismatch in perception here.

Librarians at all sizes of institutions see this gateway role as being among their primary goals, along with the licensing of electronic resources and maintaining a catalog of their resources. They expect most of their roles to rise in importance, or at least hold steady, over the next five years with some notable exceptions to be found in roles focused on nondigital materials. There are a few areas that research libraries prioritize substantially more than smaller libraries most notably the development and maintenance of special collections and several more technical tasks such as the management of datasets. Unlike other libraries, larger libraries view the licensing role as their single most important activity with less emphasis put on the gateway and catalog roles (see Figure 6). This may be a sign that leading-edge libraries are beginning to change their priorities to match those of faculty and students. Still, the mismatch in views on the gateway function is a cause for further reflection: if librarians view this function as critical, but faculty in certain disciplines find it to be declining in importance, how can libraries, individually or collectively, strategically

FIGURE 5. Percent of faculty and librarians rating the function of the library as a gateway for locating scholarly information as "very important," by discipline. 2003 data not available for librarians.

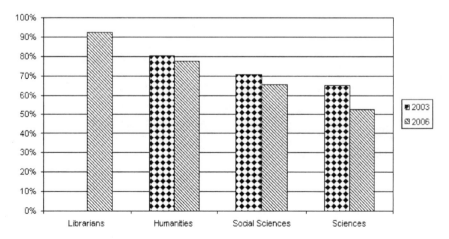

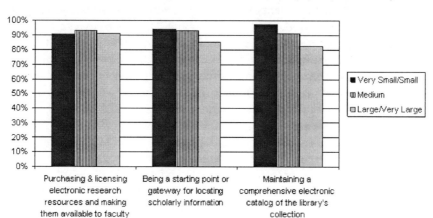

FIGURE 6. Librarians rating these functions as "very important," by size

realign the services that support the gateway function? One cannot also help but wonder if librarians have an accurate sense of faculty behaviors and attitudes.

## *Dependence on the Library*

Even as libraries plan to adapt, faculty expect to grow even less dependent on the library than they already are. This is the case across the board, although humanities scholars expect to maintain a greater dependence on the library than do social scientists, and both foresee a greater level of dependence than do scientists. Just over a quarter of scientists expect to be very dependent on libraries in five years, down from the current level of about a third. Humanists and social scientists also expect decreasing dependence over the next five years with less than 40 percent of humanists and about 30 percent of social scientists expecting continuing dependence, both drops of about five percentage points from their current levels. Again, there are some substantial differences between individual disciplines in these opinions, presumably based on particular research habits and resource availability. For example, classics scholars generally feel a substantially higher level of dependence on their libraries than do historians.

Additionally, scholars at research universities currently feel a greater level of dependence on the library than do their colleagues at small institutions, and all expect this pattern to continue into the future. While currently less than 30 percent of the faculty at very small, small, or medium sized schools are very dependent, and about 25 percent expect to be in five years, over 40 percent at large and very large schools currently feel very dependent. Although faculty at large and very large schools also expect decreasing dependence over time, they still expect a greater level of dependence than do faculty at smaller schools. This may be because larger libraries are able to offer a wider range of services.

Faculty members are growing somewhat less aware of the library's role in providing the tools and services they use in the virtual environment, and so their perceived dependence on the library is declining. In general, humanities scholars more often use tools and services closely linked to the library in their research, such as starting their search at the library itself or the library catalog, while scientists more often use tools and services that, although in some cases paid for by the library, are ultimately accessed through other means (see Figure 7). These characteristics may vary even within these broad disciplinary groups as individual disciplines may be particularly reliant on specific research methods or resources that dictate the level to which they may be oriented toward digital tools.

Perceptions of a decline in dependence are probably unavoidable as services are increasingly provided remotely, and in some ways, these shifting faculty attitudes can be viewed as a sign of library success. One

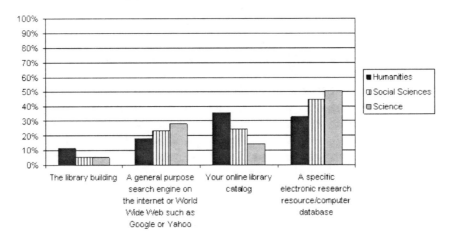

FIGURE 7. Starting points for research identified by faculty, by discipline.

can argue that they are serving faculty well, providing them with a less mediated research workflow and greater ability to perform their work more quickly and effectively. In the process, however, they may be making their own role less visible. This indicates a challenge facing libraries in the near future—as faculty needs are increasingly met without the mediation of the library, the perceived importance of the library decreases. Libraries must consider ways which they can offer new and innovative services to maintain, or in some cases recapture, the attention and support of faculty. This is an example of the way that the commercial world is washing over the academic world. All organizations in this environment must constantly innovate and improve because today's value-added service becomes tomorrow's commodity. Libraries are not immune from the need to keep identifying new ways to engage with their constituents and offer truly value-added services. This is essential if libraries are going to have a role in making researchers more effective as well as enhance the value of the library.

## THE TRANSITION AWAY FROM PRINT FOR SCHOLARLY JOURNALS

One of the most important areas on which this study sheds light is the transition away from print for scholarly journals. This is an area in which an understanding of different disciplinary needs and practices may be invaluable in guiding library response—while some disciplines are ready for this transition to take place, others simply are not. In general, libraries see a number of benefits in encouraging this transition, including anticipated space and cost savings. If pursued strategically, this transition indeed may offer substantial benefits, but if approached improperly it may prove problematic for the academy as an appropriate number of copies of important materials may not be retained for posterity.

This transition away from print has been accelerating for some time as libraries cancel the current issues of print journals in favor of electronic formats. The vast majority of libraries cancelled at least some journals in the last two years because they began a subscription to the electronic version of the journal. Faculty and librarian attitudes support the transition away from print format for the current issues of academic journals. For example, in the 2006 survey, faculty members and librarians indicate that they are generally prepared to see the library cancel the print-format version of a journal so long as it remains available in electronic format (61 percent and 63 percent agree very strongly, respectively).

Neither faculty members nor librarians are enthusiastic to see existing hard copy collections discarded, with the faculty much less enthusiastic than the librarians (20 percent and 42 percent, respectively). These preferences are relatively constant across institutional sizes but not across disciplines. Humanities scholars are especially attached to print journals, and are substantially less comfortable with their cancellation or the removal from the library of hard copy back issues (see Figure 8). There has been a decline in the share of faculty members who believe that their local library must maintain hard copy collections of journals and also a decline in the share who believe that some libraries, but not necessarily their own, must do so. Again, institutional size does not impact this belief, but discipline does. Across the board, humanities scholars are more conservative, preferring the retention of print collections in general as well as of local print collections (see Figure 9).

As discussed previously, there remain some specific disciplinary differences even among disciplinary groups—for example, philosophy scholars are generally less attached to print documents than their colleagues studying classics. We assume that these differences are related to specific disciplinary research methods and resources available, suggesting that researchers are interested in working with whatever are the most effective

FIGURE 8. Percent of faculty and librarians agreeing strongly with these statements, by discipline.

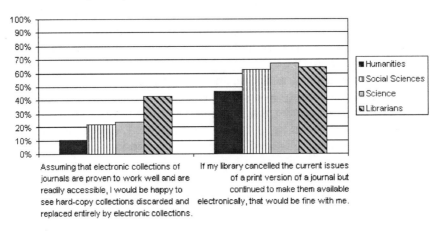

FIGURE 9. Percent of faculty agreeing strongly with the statement "Regardless of how reliable and safe electronic collections of journals are, it will always be crucial for _____ to maintain hard copy collections of journals," by discipline.

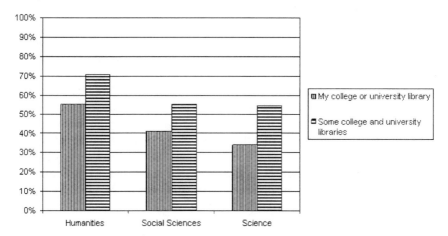

tools available to them. Certain disciplines may be primarily reliant on print, and thusly place a greater importance on maintaining print contents because print currently best matches their needs. As tools evolve, however, these researchers may migrate to digital tools that are better suited to their needs. Here one must think deeply about incentives and motivation. Is it likely that any discipline would be committed to paper for its own sake? Put another way, if there is a faster, easier, and more convenient way for a scholar to conduct his or her work, how can they resist it? As will be discussed later, economics is a field which has undergone considerable transformation, we presume in large part because of the changing resources and tools available to the field.

For many librarians, digital tools offer a number of advantages entirely aside from their potential research advantages. They may be less expensive, more easily managed, or offer space savings or decreased administrative burdens. While librarians may be eager to emphasize digital resources and move away from physical ones, clearly some disciplines will be more willing to work toward these objectives than will others. Moving aggressively to a digital platform in the sciences may not provoke much resistance, while doing so in the humanities may bring substantial faculty complaints. Digital tools offer different levels of value to different types of scholars, and libraries should target their efforts at transformation in the fields where positive attitudes and receptiveness to change already exists.

We believe that the elimination of print current issues is a fast arriving reality, perhaps faster than some libraries recognize. This transition creates a number of important system-wide issues to be addressed, which may go unnoticed by individual libraries concerned with local problems. A reliance on digital information sources means that these sources must be reliable and exist in the long term, indicating a great need for the careful attention to digital preservation. As a component of this preservation concern, it is essential that a sufficient number of print copies are maintained to serve as backups against digital losses and for the unique characteristics of the original artifact.[2] Without attention to these issues from the system-wide level, there is a significant risk that these issues will go unrecognized or unaddressed until it is too late. It is important that libraries anticipate the challenges and risks inherent in the print transition and act strategically to address them on the system level, rather than acting purely locally and allowing key concerns to go unaddressed.

## *ECONOMICS*

Although consideration of disciplinary differences is important in the crafting and provisioning of library service offerings, libraries should not assume that disciplinary patterns will remain unchanging over time. Just because a field is committed to paper or has a deep affinity for the library today does not mean it will continue to do so in the future. As tools and alternative ways to get information have become available to better serve a particular discipline, scholars' views on digital resources seem to change dramatically and rapidly. Presently, we will make this case for economics based on the data from these surveys, but it is true even in humanities disciplines. For example, in the initial years of JSTOR's existence, there was resistance to JSTOR from historians; today it is the most heavily used discipline in JSTOR. If the tools are there and valuable, they will be used.

The field of economics provides an example of how this sort of change can occur. In 2000, the attitudes of economists toward the library more closely resembled those of humanities scholars, being generally reliant on the library and on printed materials. They have since shifted dramatically, in recent years becoming more extreme than even many scientific disciplines in their feelings of independence from the library and their focus on online information resources. This change certainly relates to the particular scholarly communication patterns within this discipline but may be more broadly predictive of how research habits may shift as new resources enable research to be performed in new media.

## *Perceptions of the Library*

In the last several years, the perceptions economists hold of the library have changed substantially. Between 2003 and 2006, the percentage of economists indicating they found the library's gateway role to be very important dropped almost fifteen percentage points. In 2006, the percentage of economists who believed this gateway role to be very important was actually below the average level of scientists, falling to 48 percent. Economists also have felt their level of dependence on the library dropping even faster than they themselves anticipated. In 2003, 33 percent of economists felt very dependent on their campus library for their research, and only 25 percent expected to feel that way in five years. In fact, only three years later, only 23 percent felt very dependent on their campus library. Looking forward, less than 18 percent of economists in 2006 expected to be very dependent on their campus library by 2011 (see Figure 10).

FIGURE 10. Percent of economics faculty responding very dependent to "How dependent would you say you are on your college or university library for research you conduct?"

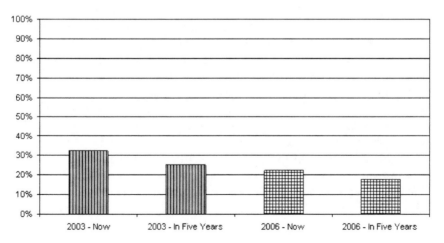

In addition to their changing perceptions of the library, the attitudes of economists regarding print and electronic resources have also changed in the last several years. For example, economics is among the disciplines least concerned with maintaining access to paper copies of journals, preferring to do their research online. Since 2003, the level of economics faculty agreeing strongly with the idea of their library canceling current issues of print journals and only providing electronic access has risen by over ten percentage points to over 70 percent. Similarly, the level of economists feeling that it will always be crucial for their library to maintain a paper collection of journals has fallen over ten percentage points to below 25 percent. This places them among the least concerned about continuing access to print materials, keeping pace with the more extreme scientific disciplines. This pattern demonstrates that as a discipline, economics has made a relatively complete conceptual transition to relying primarily (if not exclusively) on online resources. This is distinctly different from many humanists and social scientists who, even though they may do much of their regular research online, are uncomfortable with the idea of giving up access to paper copies. Unlike scholars in these disciplines, economists generally are deeply satisfied with electronic journals and are ready to transition.

## *Changing Research Patterns in Economics*

Interested in understanding how this dramatic degree of change occurred, Ithaka interviewed a number of economics scholars representing several different archetypes within the field. These interviews paint a picture of a discipline whose fundamental practices have not changed dramatically but rather have evolved to be substantially digital as structures and technologies to support this have arisen. For a variety of reasons, including the mismatch between the pace of findings in the field and long journal article gestation periods, there emerged a universally accepted practice of circulating working papers to rapidly disseminate research throughout the field. Historically, working papers have for the most part been published in local series by university departments of economics, independent research institutions, and government and multilateral agencies such as the National Bureau of Economic Research (NBER). Print copies were circulated by mail to a list of subscribers. Scholars would discover new research by browsing working paper collections held locally and by sharing recommendations and papers with their peers, a social network which served as a discovery engine as well as a means of access to papers not available locally.

This working papers network became the primary mechanism for research dissemination, with journal publication serving to validate the work, support the tenure and review process, and ensure long term preservation. It is easy to imagine, given the reliance on existing paper-based communications networks, how the networked environment has been a catalyst for swift change in this field. Research has become primarily a digital process and the Internet has lowered the barriers to the publication and sharing of working papers, allowing researchers to trivially make their work available worldwide. This has sped up considerably the publication cycle of working papers and has also reduced barriers to access—in addition to relying on one's social and scholarly network to seek out a paper of interest, researchers can get directly to a paper with a click on a link. When one finds a reference to an interesting article, very often the article can be found and accessed, either as a working paper or in its published form, as a link on the author's own Web page. It has similarly shifted the discovery process, as researchers identify works of interest through simple Web searches and alert services, rather than relying on word of mouth and widespread browsing of paper materials. In the simplest form of Web publication, economists merely upload their work to institutional repositories or their own Web space, publishing instantly. Several systems have arisen to complement or extend this self-publishing process, either by creating structures to centralize listings of works hosted by the researcher or by providing a centralized space for the posting of such working papers.

Research Papers in Economics (RePEc)[3] is an example of the first model, a free and nonprofit Web-based listing of working papers. RePEc ingests materials from a wide range of institutional repositories, allowing search and browsing of materials in a centralized listing rather than requiring the user to individually visit the homepages or relevant repositories of various researchers. Social Science Research Network (SSRN)[4] provides an example of the second type of service, allowing researchers to submit their working papers to a shared central repository. Although quite different in structure and mission (SSRN is a for-profit enterprise), both provide similar research functionality. Users of either service gain immediate access to the latest working papers and can search or browse by keyword or author to facilitate discovery. In addition, each offers alert services, which notify scholars when new papers matching a custom set of criteria are found, allowing a researcher to keep up to date on the latest works on topics of interest. Both also offer a variety of supplemental tools and functions, including measurements of popularity that may be used both as a discovery tool, spotlighting what is being widely read in the field, and as a measurement of quality, monitoring how widely read and cited a particular paper is. Although such metrics have not taken over as tools for tenure and promotion decisions, there is the potential that if they are found reliable enough, they may supplant traditional journal-based measurements.

These shifts demonstrate how changes in the resources available can change the medium of research without necessarily changing the practices involved. The shift to primarily online research did not occur because economists altered their habits or experienced changes in their research needs. The fundamental needs and practices of economists remained steady, but the environment changed to allow these needs to be met in a different medium than was historically possible. As economists realized the potential of the Internet to meet their information needs, and as structures and tools were developed to facilitate their traditional practices, economists found that they were able accomplish the same work using a different set of tools. In fact, this new set of tools allowed economists to be more efficient and effective in their existing practices, removing many of the barriers imposed by traditional print-based communications.

## *Opportunities for Change*

Although these changing practices have generally made economists less dependent on traditional library services, they can also offer an opportunity to learn new ways the library can invest resources and offer value. We have been somewhat surprised in our conversations by how little direct interaction there is between faculty and librarians. In this dynamic environment, lack of direct engagement with faculty could be disastrous for libraries. Understanding that engaging the faculty is not an easy task, it would seem a worthy goal to focus efforts on engaging this important discipline. Economists may not be relying on traditional library services, but by engaging with this group the library may be able to identify and develop innovative services to complement their existing digital practices. Furthermore, as was evident in the survey data, these changing practices make economists natural partners to explore the potential benefits of reallocating scarce resources by removing legacy print collections or otherwise phasing out unused traditional services.

## RECOMMENDATIONS

### Compete to Be Valuable

Libraries need to accept, indeed embrace, the fact that they are operating in a competitive environment. The information landscape has changed since the time when the library was the only real venue for research available to scholars. Researchers now use a wide variety of nonlibrary research tools, ranging from mass-market tools such as Google to tailored disciplinary services such as RePEc, to meet their information needs. The library must identify those needs that are adequately met by nonlibrary services and focus their energy on information needs and services that are not being addressed adequately. This is where the library can add value. There may be situations in which nonlocally provided solutions are equally or better able to support the research needs of faculty, and libraries should not see these as threats but as opportunities; if a system-wide solution such as RePEc satisfies the needs of economists, for example, the library may be most valuable by crafting service offerings to complement, rather than compete with, such solutions. In other areas, however, a locally provided solution may be able to offer superior service. Libraries should also consider very carefully any services that seem to benefit from face-to-face interaction. This is an area where being local is a distinct competitive advantage. In any event, libraries must develop a better understanding of what faculty truly value and craft services that address these needs.

### Understand Changing Faculty Needs

If the library is to act strategically in a competitive environment, it must develop and maintain a thorough understanding of the needs of its important constituents. Although Ithaka's survey work aims to paint a picture of changing faculty attitudes and needs system-wide, libraries must also seek to understand local needs and priorities. While formal surveys such as these may be excessive on the local level, engaging closely with faculty across the campus will enhance the library's understanding of the particular needs and concerns of their own faculty. Both the library leadership as well as individual librarians, formally and informally, should be reaching out to faculty members to understand the nature of their teaching and research projects and how their needs are being met and could be met better. This is not a new or particularly enlightened idea, and we are aware of numerous efforts at research libraries to engage more closely with faculty,[5] but it is such an important point that it is worthy of emphasis. We are also aware of institutions where precious little of this goes on, a situation that really should be corrected.

## Engage Faculty in the Change Process

Deeper engagement with faculty offers the opportunity for the library to work in collaboration with faculty to achieve particular outcomes, rather than simply on their behalf. Engaging in discussion with faculty will provide the conduit to better understand each other's needs and perspectives and make it possible for faculty and librarians to work together effectively. The example of economics comes to mind, where economics faculty seem prepared for changing policies related to storage of print materials, a perspective that could very well mesh with objectives of the library. Developing together a well conceived plan for making the transition would benefit all parties.

## Consider Disciplinary Differences

One important lesson to be learned from these data is that different disciplines have dramatically different needs, interests, and priorities. In their planning, libraries should recall that different disciplines have widely varying reliance on traditional materials, and the digital tools necessary for effective work in a particular discipline may simply be lacking. While emphasizing that digital tools may offer savings and efficiency to libraries, and they may be welcomed enthusiastically in certain disciplines, it may be unrealistic to expect humanities scholars to keep pace with their scientist colleagues in this process. Those disciplines that are more enthusiastic users of digital resources may pose different challenges than those which are not. Highly digital scholars may disintermediate the library from their research process entirely, leaving the library with the challenge of remaining relevant and offering value-added services to meet the faculty's new needs. These same disciplines, however, may offer the best opportunities for change as they may be enthusiastic partners with the library in new endeavors or in efforts to reclaim space by removing print collections. While libraries may be less concerned with disciplines still reliant on traditional research processes, these offer libraries the task of understanding why digital tools are not meeting their needs and of identifying ways to create and offer digital resources which will be of value to these scholars. As we saw in the case of economics, however, the relationship of disciplinary research habits to the library should not be assumed to be fixed. Changing availability of resources may cause substantial shifts in these more traditional disciplines' research patterns, and libraries should be certain to be at least aware of, if not leading, these shifts.

## CONCLUSION

The information environment of higher education is shifting rapidly, presenting libraries with unique challenges and opportunities. As we have seen in the field of economics, the availability of new digital information resources can prompt dramatic shifts in the way faculty in a discipline relate to and use the library. In this dynamic environment —an environment where libraries compete with commercial resources like Google —it is essential that libraries operate in a strategic fashion. They cannot simply continue to operate as they have in the past.

Libraries should invest continuously in research to understand the needs of their faculty. By better understanding the needs of faculty, libraries will be able to anticipate their requirements and identify the services the library can offer that are not addressed by networked resources. Only with such information can libraries adapt proactively, leading faculty to improved and more efficient research practices while freeing up resources for other activities. Certain disciplines, like economics, are on the vanguard of using electronic resources in transformative ways and offer libraries the ability to experience the future. Investing in understanding the needs of faculty in such disciplines can serve as a guide to help the libraries develop new strategies for success in a world of digital scholarly communications. A library that is able to anticipate the changing information needs of its constituent faculty will be better able to maintain its position of relevance in the university.

## NOTES

1. The purchaser role was described in the survey by the statement "the library pays for resources I need, from academic journals to books to electronic databases," the archive role by "the library serves as a repository of resources—in other words, it archives, preserves, and keeps track of resources," and the gateway role by "the library is a starting point or 'gateway' for locating information for my research."

2. Ithaka is currently engaged in a study in partnership with UC Berkeley to determine the levels of print maintenance necessary to meet future community needs.

3. See http://repec.org/.

4. See http://www.ssrn.com/, and http://www.ssrn.com/ern/index.html for the Economics Research Network section of the site.

5. Perhaps some of the best examples of library-faculty collaboration have come in the area of information literacy programs. Librarians have worked together with faculty to develop programs which complement faculty pedagogic goals and teach essential principles of information discovery, evaluation, and use. The most successful programs recognize the need for close collaboration between faculty and librarians to create programs which integrate information literacy training meaningfully into the curriculum. See Andrea L. Foster, "Information Navigation 101," *The Chronicle of Higher Education*, March 9, 2007; Thomas P. Mackey and Trudi E. Jacobson, "Information literacy: a collaborative endeavor," *College Teaching* 53, no. 4 (2005); and James Hooks et al., "Information literacy for branch campuses and branch libraries," *Library Philosophy and Practice*, October 1, 2007.

# Unintended Consequences: A Friendly User Looks at User-Friendly Digitization

Jack A. Siggins

**ABSTRACT.** Growth in digital capacity and other technological advances have placed us on the cusp of great cultural transformation. As we race headlong into this future, rapid innovation, followed by equally rapid obsolescence, challenges academic administrators who must make decisions involving technology that make them uneasy. This article discusses the implications of some of the major changes in academic technology and identifies possible pitfalls for research libraries arising from this transformation.

In 2007, Peter Gruenberg of Germany and Albert Fert of France were jointly awarded the Nobel Prize in Physics for a major discovery regarding giant magnetoresistance. Their remarkable success ten years prior to the award in this rather arcane area of science revolutionized the ways we communicate and store information. Their discovery made it possible for you to have the pocket-sized iPod that probably sits quietly in your purse or pocket and for all of us to have almost instantaneous access to a vast array of databases and sources of information.

The purpose of this paper, however, is not to heap praise on these two exceptional individuals, no matter how well-deserved it might be, but instead to take a closer look at some of the implications and challenges,

---

Jack A. Siggins is University Librarian, The George Washington University, Washington, DC.

both positive and negative, these and other extraordinary technological advances present to our society and the world. We can do this by looking at events over the last few years, identifying trends they suggest, and projecting them into the future.

Some of the questions to be explored are: What is the nature of the interaction between this technology and our society thus far and what is it likely to be? Who will be the losers and gainers as a result of this new technology?

Thomas Friedman in his book, *The World Is Flat*, claims that speed and ease of access to digital information sources have improved prospects of people in less-developed countries, not just modernized societies. Certainly, over the last decade, we have seen significant growth in the uses of technology in our own world of academic and research libraries. Instructional use of course management software, such as Blackboard, has escalated from an interesting curiosity to an absolute necessity, even among faculty who only a few years ago were loathe to acknowledge its pedagogical value, let alone try to learn how to use it. Today, university instructional programs are regularly judged by both students and administrators alike for the quantity and quality of their use of educational technology.

As all of us are aware, Google is heavily involved in a historic and ambitious effort to make the full text of all of the world's books searchable and accessible online. The self-described purpose of the Google Book Search project is to build an index to all books in the world. The comprehensiveness established for the Google Book Search Project seeks nothing less than the ability for any of us connected to the Web with a computer to find any book. Because only about an estimated 10 percent of all books ever published are still in print, Google must work with large libraries, in addition to publishers.

In February 2008, the University of Michigan at Ann Arbor proudly announced that their joint project with Google to scan their entire library holdings had reached an important milestone, namely, that the one millionth volume had just been completed. That leaves only 6.5 million more to go. As we all know, Michigan is one of several major libraries around the world engaged through contractual relationships with Google in attaining the expressed objective of making full texts of millions of books widely accessible electronically. In contrast to other organizations, however, Michigan is one of only a few that has agreed to scan all of its holdings, including those still covered by copyright.

Carnegie Mellon University announced in November 2007 that it has scanned, digitized, and cataloged 1.5 million books and has made about half of them available free online. Most of the work for its "Million Book Project" is actually being done overseas in China, India, and Egypt, thus spreading the largess from their project to these developing economies as well. Unfortunately, a large part of the collection being scanned is still under copyright, with the result that only about 10% of the scanned books can be made available online.

Cornell University's library joined the Google Book Search project in the summer of 2007 and began to digitize the first 500,000 titles from its collection. Both copyrighted and public-domain items will be scanned. Full texts of those publications with no copyright restrictions will be accessible on-line. Only title, author, and access information will be available for copyrighted items.

Microsoft, not about to let the competition get a large advantage, has undertaken similar efforts to engage in massive digitizing projects. Both Google and Microsoft know that these sorts of efforts proclaiming to make books widely accessible to millions of readers around the world generate a great deal of excitement, especially among librarians. The idea of open access to enormous amounts of information stirs up the feeling among librarians that maybe at long last their usually unstated utopian desire to make all information available at any time to everyone is almost in reach.

Google and Microsoft claim to be motivated by what they see as demand for instant access arising from the "I-want-it-now" generation of young users. Academic librarians tend to confirm this trend as they come to realize that the majority of students nowadays begin their scholarly inquiries with a search of Google. Google's efforts seem to be paying off, at least in terms of growing popularity. Last year, the Centre for Learning and Performance Technologies listed Google and Google Scholar in the top 100 favorite information retrieval tools among professors and e-learning experts. Included on the list are web-browsers, RSS feeders, blog programs, Power Point software, and e-mail clients.

But what about content? Large-scale book-scanning projects run by both commercial and noncommercial organizations are steadily making books available in a form that, not only is easier to access, but also allows queries and interpretations. These resources have the potential to make possible research that previously was difficult and remote. They also raise the possibility of addressing the problem of the exorbitant cost of textbooks.

Publishers are making textbooks longer and more comprehensive, but also more expensive. Most students cannot afford to purchase all the books assigned to them each semester. At least one publisher, McGraw-Hill, has recognized this problem and is exploring content-licensing arrangements with colleges and universities to allow digital delivery of the intellectual content of textbooks electronically rather than in printed form.

A great deal of hype about the benefits to students and faculty engaged in the teaching and learning processes has been generated. In the give and take of classroom instruction and individual and group learning, at least three assumptions seem to be present. One is that students want more technology that will make it easier for faculty to deliver and students to receive whatever is being passed along in the instruction and learning process. Another is that although initially reluctant to adopt new technological innovations and tools, most faculty now feel at ease with them and are using them increasingly as part of their pedagogical repertoire. A third assumption is that students regularly avail themselves of these new technologies because using them saves time and because the technologies are presented in terms the students are used to and with which they feel most comfortable. In the minds of some proponents of this technology, speed and ease of access to digitized resources have come to equal better and more thorough learning. The unspoken promise is that the more sophisticated the technology and the easier the access to it, the better the learning experience will be.

Last year a survey of over nine hundred academic faculty was released purporting to show that half of those surveyed preferred electronic resources, compared to only 18 percent who preferred print versions. Another conclusion from the survey was that faculty wanted portable reading devices and more electronic content. These seemingly important implications were somewhat deflated by the fact that the survey was conducted by Ebrary, the e-book company, using the company website and its list of users.

A similar assumption about the force and promise of digitization and technical innovations has led to open verbal warfare between some very distinguished literary figures on the one hand and the most outspoken proponents of the conversion to virtual bookshelves on the other. One infamous instance of this confrontation appeared in 2006 at BookExpo America, the annual publishing convention that brings together thousands of literati, book lovers and publishing industry representatives to display, celebrate, and discuss developments in the world of publishing. The catalyst was an article written by Kevin Kelly, the guru of the online magazine, *Wired*. In his article, which ironically was printed in the *New York Times Magazine*, Kelly asserted the position that he has long promoted: the inevitability of the steady progression toward the total capturing of all human knowledge in digital form and its compression onto an easily transportable, hand-held device. This evokes again the notion that maybe the librarians' utopian dream will come true after all. In his 1994 book, *Out of Control*, Kelly had taken the position that the human brain did not function in an organized structure so much as in a chaotic but interrelated collection of components.

The primary combatant at the 2006 BookExpo Convention was none other than John Updike, the Harvard-educated author of numerous successful and honored volumes of poems, fiction, and essays. His target was not the assembled book publishers and booksellers arrayed before him, but rather the promoters of technological information and access who, as he described them, derided the protections and conventions of authorship and copyright. Kelly in particular was singled out for Updike's derision.

Several months later, at her speech accepting the 2007 Nobel Prize in Literature, Doris Lessing took up where Updike left off. Lessing bemoaned what she described as the fragmenting culture we find ourselves in today. It is a culture in which young men and women have years of education in schools and universities but know little of the world; they have read comparatively little; and their only specialty is what they have gained through computers and blogging on the Internet. Promoters of technology, on the other hand, counter this complaint by arguing that digitization and wide-spread network access will make reading a broad range of literature more possible throughout the world, especially in the poorer countries that today have little or no access to printed books.

Even France has gotten into the argument. In the summer of 2007, the president of the *Bibliotheque Nationale* criticized Google's book digitization project on the grounds that it would only promote American cultural domination of the world.

Without taking a position in this argument, it is reasonable to say that both sides present strong cases for their respective views of the future. It is also safe to say that future developments very likely will not result in complete vindication for either side, but will instead settle somewhere in between the two pictured extremes. Technological advancements will inevitably occur one on top of another, but one only has to look at the melancholy record of claims by technology enthusiasts in the past to get a more balanced perspective of what might happen. Television did not destroy radio. Computers have not driven students away from libraries. The Internet has not made librarians unnecessary.

The value of innovative technology has oftentimes been exaggerated by its enthusiastic supporters, especially when the technology has just been introduced. As a result, today a healthy skepticism arises among many persons when a new technological breakthrough is proclaimed to have such a profound and immediate impact that the previous technology is instantaneously made obsolete, unnecessary, and antediluvian by comparison.

One experience with which I am familiar illustrates this phenomenon. Several years ago, a newly arrived chancellor at a large university announced to the library senior administrators that the library would not need stacks for books any more because the wide availability of microfilm would allow all publications to be converted to reels of film, allowing the books to be discarded. We all know how off the mark that prediction turned out to be. This same chancellor had been trained as a physicist, so perhaps his inflated view of the power of technology may be excused. He later, however, tried to absorb the library's computer system that handled circulation and cataloging into the main university computer system with exactly the same disastrous results for the university that the librarians had predicted.

The growing and creative uses of the Web also put an enormous strain on the ability of technicians and innovators to keep up with demand for bandwidth. Streaming video, file-sharing, and other services have placed a heavy burden on the Internet's infrastructure. Phone and cable companies are being pressed to spend billions of dollars for improvements. Other modern countries, such as Japan and most European nations, have already addressed this problem of capacity, with the result that their citizens have far greater Internet services than citizens in the United States. With this prospect hanging over them, Congress is being pressed to do something about the looming bandwidth collapse. At the same time, telecommunication corporations are using the threat of a collapse of the Web as a cudgel to get what the industry really wants, which is to have the industry deregulated so the corporations can charge the public whatever they wish. News reports regularly chronicle dire warnings from Verizon and AT&T that the cost to the nation of expanding and upgrading capacity will cost billions of dollars.

Much of the attention and planning for a national cyberinfrastructure has focused on Large-Scale Digitization Initiatives (LSDI) and their ability to provide digital access to a wide range of materials. Less energy has been given to the concomitant issue of preservation of digital archives. Thus far, this technical challenge has been somewhat pushed aside by the euphoria derived from the excitement of being involved in big projects and the comparative ease with which the technical issues arising from access seem to have been resolved to this point. The longitudinal problems of storage and preservation of digital resources are actually part of the access issue, but participating institutions have found it necessary to make compromises regarding preservation quality standards in order to reduce storage costs. They have found it much more rewarding instead to promote the more gratifying promise of immediate access.

The digitization of journals and databases presents other problems for potential users. Although interlibrary loan has been a useful resource for researchers for many years, users at small- or medium-sized libraries today are often handicapped because their institution cannot afford to subscribe to databases owned by corporations. At present, individuals cannot purchase access to databases even if they can afford it. Full-text services, such as JSTOR and ProQuest, are unavailable to a large group of potential users. Users can consult indices to find out if an article or database exists, but if a full text version is wanted, the user's choices are often limited to doing without, using the old-fashioned method of visiting the physical or electronic repository of the collection itself, or as an increasingly large number of scholars are doing, prevailing upon the good will of friends and colleagues at large research institutions with larger library resources to obtain the full text version of a publication for them.

Google has made it clear that its goal for Google Book Search is to build a comprehensive index of all the books of the world. For another project, Google Publishing Partners, Google works with more than ten thousand international publishers to provide information about copyright-protected books, including samples of text, to everyone on the Web. As already mentioned, there is the Google Library Project, which has as its aim the digitization of as many books as possible.

These monumental efforts, however, have other problems as well. Questions have been raised about whether these resources are being organized in the best way necessary to meet the needs of modern researchers. In 2007, The Andrew Mellon Foundation awarded a grant to the Council on Library and Information Resources to study this very issue. Sometime users of Google Book Search can miss items when unusual spellings in older texts are not considered. Pages can be missed or placed out of order in scanning. Sometimes catalog information is wrong, and keyword terms are inaccurate. Such problems suggest that the promises and assumptions engendered by the excitement of technological breakthroughs may turn out to be something much less, perhaps characterized by a hodgepodge of databases and interfaces leading to collections of books not so well organized in a user-friendly manner.

Nonetheless, many students and faculty benefit from the advancement in digitization and expanding capabilities of the Web. A growing number of universities provide online courses and programs leading to advanced degrees. These allow students to improve their skills and academic qualifications with minimum face-to-face contact. Some have pointed out, however, that such remote courses of instruction seem to be less well suited for humanities classes and seminars where face-to-face discussions between people conversing around a table or in a classroom are more effective.

Another question, of course, is who will benefit most in the long run from these massive digitization efforts and the move to technology-enhanced learning. This is a very important question to keep asking ourselves as we engage these new technologies. Control of content and access to digitized collections today are major battlegrounds for authors, researchers, librarians, and publishers, each of whom has a vested interest in the terms and conditions under which these resources are made available. Authors, although less concerned about profits, still want to be certain their rights of authorship are protected, while insuring access to their work for other researchers. Researchers want easy access to the publications of other scholars. Librarians want to observe the rights of authorship and promote the publishing of materials, while making everything available with as little cost and as few restrictions as possible. Publishers want to do whatever is necessary to maintain a certain level of corporate profits.

For many decades, these four elements worked cooperatively when the source was available only on paper and when access was limited by time and distance. With the rising costs related to print publishing and the arrival of digitization, the Web, and easier forms of communication, new challenges to this arrangement appeared. Corporations saw a real chance to increase profitability by gaining control over access to journals and databases. Monopolies and oligopolies formed that gathered sole control over publications in the hands of large, usually international, corporations.

The Google projects, in particular, present yet another potentially ominous prospect. Many librarians are concerned about turning over so much control of the digital conversion of books to large, powerful, profit-oriented corporations that restrict access and forbid their library partners from even revealing the terms of their contracts. They ask, "What will happen if Google decides to take advantage of their dominance in order to maximize their profits?" The specter of experiences with Wiley, Elsevier, Springer-Verlag, and other journal dealers appears in their minds.

Some librarians recall when in the late 1980s even OCLC, the friendliest and most important utility for libraries around the world, tried to claim sole ownership of the copyright to the OCLC database, despite the fact that the sources of the information in the database were the libraries themselves. Fortunately, OCLC backed down from its claim in the face of opposition and challenges from member libraries, and with a change in senior management, OCLC regained its corporate senses and gradually regained its standing in the library community. In addition to coming away with a feeling of having been betrayed, however, many librarians learned a real life lesson about corporate perspective, if not out-and-out greed.

The Association of American Publishers (AAP) has presented a different set of challenges. In 2007, the AAP launched PRISM, which stands for the "Partnership for Research Integrity in Science and Medicine." Ostensibly created to "safeguard the scientific and medical peer-review process," PRISM is actually intended to block efforts to promote open access. It is aimed primarily at policy makers in the government and Congress. Its stated goals match perfectly with the public relations campaign of the AAP and in particular with the AAP's attacks against the National Institutes of Health's Public Access Policy.

Within a short time after PRISM was launched, many in the academic and research community reacted with denunciations and outrage. Some publishers and journal editors made it clear they did not agree with PRISM's views on public access and open access. Researchers called upon their colleagues to convey their objections to those publishers aligning themselves with PRISM by refusing to submit reviews and articles or serve as editors. Several AAP members, including some prominent university presses, made it abundantly clear that they disagreed with both the message and the purpose of PRISM. Within a week, the AAP had backed off by changing the stated purpose of PRISM appearing on its website from a confrontational posture to a more conciliatory message. It now professes to seek new models to expand access for both subscribers and nonsubscribers, while ensuring the quality and economic viability of peer-reviewed journals.

Increasingly complex systems introduced without careful consideration of their implications will inevitably produce unexpected consequences. Warnings, if not flaws, in the systems we use appear regularly. For example, in February 2008, a group of researchers at Princeton University announced that they have discovered a way to steal encrypted information stored on computer hard disks by applying the ingeniously simple technique of chilling a computer chip with a blast of frigid air. This blast of frigid air can come from as common a source as an aerosol can of dust remover.

Today, nearly all compositions begin in digital format. By 2009, manufacturers will make available terabyte scale hard drives. Faced by this new capacity, librarians will need to play an even more active role in determining what data is preserved and take steps now to be sure that the information is accurate and relevant to the needs of current and future researchers. They also must consider carefully what impact digitization may have on our culture and on writing itself.

Google is an example of how technology has altered our personal and academic lives. Although digitization is nothing new to libraries, Google's influence is derived from the scope of its vision and the audacity of its undertaking. The question about the future that needs to be answered, however, is whether the corporate vision really matches the needs of the public for unlimited access to relatively inexpensive and widely available information that is the foundation of our democracy.

As digitization grows at a rapidly accelerating pace and librarians struggle to keep ahead of demand from users for improved access to the vast resources available via the Web, it is important that librarians and researchers be alert to the implications of the creeping concentration of control of information resources in the hands of corporate conglomerates. One response to the Google question is the Open Content Alliance (OCA). The OCA initiative is largely self-funded; libraries that join are required to pay the cost of scanning the books. The scanned items are stored at the Internet Archive and are available from its website.

After its start by Brewster Kahle, the OCA quickly was joined by more than eighty research libraries and research institutions. It is seen as an alternative to the Google effort and to the concern about having so much control of access to the digitized collections in the hands of one corporation. In contrast to Google, the OCA effort focuses on books not covered by copyright restrictions. Interestingly, Google's biggest commercial competitors, Microsoft and Yahoo, have signed on to OCA, although Microsoft, perhaps confirming that its motive is not totally altruistic, later added a restrictive clause to the agreement with OCA that prohibits a book it has digitized from being included in commercial search engines.

In 1996, Alan Greenspan, former Chairman of the Federal Reserve Board, first used the phrase, "irrational exuberance," to describe an overvalued stock market and unduly escalated asset values. As we know, his analysis was followed by drastic slumps in stock markets around the world. What Greenspan was referring to was the herding tendency that appears in human beings when we have inadequate knowledge and information about an important occurrence and feel the need to act in response. In those situations, we often use the behavior of others as a guide to our own decisions, especially if these individuals or institutions have prominent standing in our community. Their ideas and actions are intuitively appealing because they seemingly match our own thoughts and values. Their explanations become the basis of our own rationale that may evolve into the commonly accepted wisdom on the matter without being thoroughly challenged or thought through.

Promotion of technology can act like a contagion, spreading unchecked and unverified as limitations and consequences are ignored in favor of the chase. As communication has increased with the expansion of the Internet, the feedback mechanisms that should make leaders wary of bad decisions has given way to the herding instinct and the somewhat comforting thought that if miscalculations are made, other leaders at least will be in the same boat. The director of the library at one participant in the Google digitization program brushed aside concerns about copyright issues arising from that institution's massive digitizing project by citing the Fair Use clause of the copyright law. Whether this interpretation will turn out to be correct or avoid costly litigation remains to be seen. This uncertainty has nonetheless failed to discourage library directors at some other major institutions from leaping into the same void.

In the world of libraries, the rush to join Google's projects may be the library version of Greenspan's "Irrational Exuberance." The lesson for librarians is that efforts to digitize huge collections are both a defining moment in the history of libraries and a major challenge. Library administrators in particular must be certain that they fully understand the ramifications of their decisions before they act.

Change is the fuel of technology, but it also brings an extraordinary array of complicated challenges and decisions. George Noory, the host of the late night radio show, "Coast to Coast AM," in a program describing how the ancient Mayans viewed the impact of change in the future, advised his listeners to be prepared, not scared.

In the same way, librarians should prepare for future applications of digitization and technology by fully understanding their implications, developing an expertise in their uses, assuming a skeptical view of their significance, and by becoming actively engaged in determining who they will be presented to and how they will be presented. If they do that, librarians will likely be better prepared to predict accurately and deal effectively with problems that everyone else will consider to be unintended consequences.

# From Advocacy to Implementation: The NIH Public Access Policy and Its Impact

Heather Dalterio Joseph

**ABSTRACT.** On December 26, 2007, President Bush signed the Consolidated Appropriations Act of 2008[1] into law. The bill contained language requiring all investigators funded by the National Institutes of Health (NIH) to place a copy of manuscripts resulting from NIH-funded research into the National Library of Medicine's online repository, PubMed Central, to be made publicly available within one year of publication in a peer-reviewed journal. The policy will take effect April 7, 2008, and will impact three constituencies on college and university campuses: NIH-funded investigators; institutional research administrators and legal counsel; and librarians. This paper will explore the new policy's requirements of each constituency, the roles each may consider playing to ensure effective compliance with the policy, and the new opportunities that are afforded to all of the three groups by this groundbreaking initiative.

## THE ISSUE—WHY PUBLIC ACCESS?

The relatively recent proliferation of policies—institutional, national and international—calling for greater access to the results of research conducted using public funds has its roots in several places. In general, governments invest in scientific research with the expectation that it will

---

Heather Dalterio Joseph is Executive Director, The Scholarly Publishing and Academic Resources Coalition (SPARC), Washington, DC.

result in improvements to the public good; that it will spur the advancement of scientific discovery, lead to greater innovation and, ultimately, that it will create economic stimulus. Funders have increasingly recognized that dissemination is an essential component of the research process and that the research cannot rightly be considered complete unless the results are communicated to others. They recognize that the process of conducting research is a cumulative one that can only advance through sharing results. The value of an investment in research is maximized only through use—when findings are shared and built upon by others.

Too often, however, the results of this research are simply not available to the wide community of potential users. They remain locked behind journal subscriptions that may not be affordable and gated behind barriers that do not allow them to be accessed or linked with other resources. While it was taken for granted for decades that this type of system was the most advantageous—in a research environment that was largely paper-based—it is no longer optimal, nor desirable, in the current digital networked world. The Internet provides us with new opportunities to bring information to a much broader audience at virtually no additional cost and also to use it in new and innovative ways.

The culmination of these types of pressures has inspired a call for a new framework for sharing research, one that is designed to allow results to be more easily and more broadly accessed, shared, and used—and for policies to drive and govern the institution of such a framework. This sentiment was succinctly encapsulated in a 2005 report on scientific publishing by the International Organization for Economic Cooperation and Development, which noted, "Governments would boost innovation and get a better return on their investment in publicly funded research by making research findings more widely available.... And by doing so, they would maximize social returns on public investments."[2] Over the past several years, policies calling for greater access to the results of publicly funded research have emerged in geopolitically diverse areas, from the United States to the United Kingdom, Australia to the European Union, and beyond. These policies share striking similarities in both their goals and the language used to articulate those goals. Wherever the policies emerge, they are generally designed to:

- *Improve information access and sharing*—enable fast, free electronic access to research results.
- *Accelerate the pace of research*—create a rich resource for scientists to access research quickly and freely, and to use in new and innovative ways.

- *Enable this level of access for this and future generations of researchers*—create a permanently accessible archive of results.
- *Reduce systemic costs and eliminate inefficiencies*—reduce barriers and redundancies.
- *Improve the accountability of public funders of research*—provide a mechanism to manage research portfolios more effectively and transparently.

## THE NIH PUBLIC ACCESS POLICY

The NIH Public Access Policy certainly embraces these goals. The policy itself is quite brief, and reads:

> The Director of the National Institutes of Health shall require that all investigators funded by the NIH submit or have submitted for them to the National Library of Medicine's PubMed Central an electronic version of their final, peer-reviewed manuscripts upon acceptance for publication, to be made publicly available no later than 12 months after the official date of publication; Provided, that the NIH shall implement the public access policy in a manner consistent with copyright law.
> —Public Law 110–161, Division G, Title II, Section 218[3]

The policy applies to articles that are accepted for publication in journals on or after April 7, 2008 and to all articles that are a result of direct funding from a NIH grant or cooperative agreement, NIH contract, direct funding from a NIH intramural program, and to articles that are the work of a NIH employee.

## WHO DOES THE NIH PUBLIC ACCESS POLICY IMPACT?

The policy most directly impacts three broad categories of constituents:

- NIH-funded researchers
- University administrators (research administrators and legal counsel)
- The library community (including repository managers).

## ENSURING COMPLIANCE WITH THE POLICY

Compliance with the NIH Public Access Policy requires four basic actions:

1. Ensuring that the rights needed to deposit a manuscript into PubMed Central (PMC) have been properly reserved.
2. Ensuring that the manuscript is physically deposited into PubMed Central and subsequently approved for public availability.
3. Ensuring that an appropriate embargo period (0–12 months) is properly set.
4. Ensuring that articles are properly cited in subsequent NIH applications, proposals, and progress reports.

Each constituency—researcher, administrator, and librarian—has the potential to play a role in ensuring that these four actions are carried out properly and efficiently.

## ROLES FOR RESEARCHERS

### Retaining Necessary Rights

Before a manuscript can be deposited into the PubMed Central database, the grantee is responsible for ensuring that he or she has secured the rights necessary to do so. This process can be greatly facilitated up front by researchers proactively considering the current copyright policies of the journals with which they choose to publish their works. There are many journals that have policies that allow researchers to retain the rights necessary to comply with the NIH policy. Some journal publishers make it even easier for the researcher by going a step further and handling the deposition of the article as well. However, there are other journal publishers whose current policies implicitly prohibit researchers from complying with the NIH Public Access Policy.

Rather than struggling to determine whether a journal's policy allows compliance with the NIH policy once an article has already been accepted for publication, researchers may choose to become familiar with the journal's copyright policy *before* submitting articles for possible publication. Researchers can read the journal's policy prior to submitting an article by checking with the SHERPA/ROMEO or JULIET[4] databases or their university counsel to see if the journal's policy enables compliance. If they continue to have questions, authors may talk to the publisher directly. This provides a good opportunity to express to the publisher the importance of flexible copyright policies that balance the needs of all stakeholders in the academic and research community.

If, upon reading the policy and the copyright transfer agreement requested by the publisher, a researcher determines additional rights are needed to allow him or her to successfully comply with the NIH, he or she has several options available.

First, researchers can check in with their institution's Office of Sponsored Research or Legal Counsel to determine if the institution has a preferred mechanism for copyright compliance. (A recently published white paper on options for copyright compliance and the NIH policy from SPARC/Science Commons/ARL may be a helpful resource to these offices.[5]

Copyright transfer agreements are contracts and, as such, may be modified by either party. To ensure compliance with the NIH policy, researchers may consider modifying the copyright transfer agreement in any one of several ways to ensure they reserve rights needed:

- The first option is for the author to consider inserting NIH-suggested language into the publishers' copyright agreement. The language is simple, straightforward, and reads: "Journal acknowledges that Author retains the right to provide a copy of the final manuscript to the NIH... for public archiving in PubMed Central... no later than 12 months after publication by Journal."[6]
- A second option is for researchers to use language provided to them by their institution. Many universities are developing, adapting, or adopting addenda for researchers to append to the copyright transfer agreements requested by publishers.
- A third option is to use the SPARC Author Addendum or another of the addenda that may be generated using the Scholar's Copyright Addendum Engine (SCAE).[7] These addenda are acceptable, legally vetted tools that will facilitate compliance with the NIH public access policy.

The SPARC addendum and the addenda generated by the SCAE offer options to retain additional rights beyond simply depositing a manuscript into PubMed Central—creating an important opportunity for researchers to exploit the benefits of retaining the rights necessary to ensure the broadest practical exposure for their articles.

Having secured the rights needed to deposit a manuscript into PubMed Central, researchers have several options to ensure that the manuscript is properly uploaded:

- Individuals may deposit their manuscripts directly into PubMed Central. The NIH, which has been accepting manuscripts from individuals via their NIHMS system for nearly three years, estimates that it takes an individual, on average, less than ten minutes to successfully complete the deposition process.[8]
- A researcher can also, according to the language of the policy, have a third party submit the manuscript. This means that someone from the author's team or local institution (an assistant, co-author, grants officer, librarian, repository manager, etc.), or a publisher may carry out the initial deposit of the accepted manuscript on behalf of the author.

One thing that it is critical to note is that in all of the above cases, no matter who carries out the initial deposit of the manuscript, *the author must review and approve the article* before it can be made public and before the terms of compliance with the policy are fulfilled.

The only exception to this is if a researcher chooses to publish in a journal that has an agreement with PubMed Central to deposit all or some of their published articles into the repository on researchers' behalf. The NIH Web site contains a listing of over 300 journals that currently do this for their authors. The NIH considers publication in one of these journals sufficient to meet the compliance criteria of the policy, and the author need take no further action.[9]

## *Setting the Embargo Period*

Once a manuscript has been submitted, and is approved to be made public, the author can set the embargo period for the article—the delay before which the article will become freely available to the public. The NIH Public Access Policy allows a researcher to select an embargo period of zero to twelve months. The researcher should request the shortest embargo period appropriate for his or her discipline to help underscore the community's desire for prompt access to this critical information.

## *Proper Citation of Articles*

The final item to which a researcher must pay attention to fully comply with the policy is ensuring that articles are properly cited. When citing an article in NIH applications, proposals, and progress reports as of May 25, 2008, authors must include the PubMed Central reference number (PMCID) at the end of the citation.[10]

Although failure to comply will not be a factor in the evaluation of applications, NIH notes that it "may delay or prevent awarding of funds"—an incentive to ensure that this final step is properly completed.

## *IMPACT ON RESEARCHERS*

While the responsibility for complying with the requirements of the NIH Public Access Policy falls most squarely on the shoulders of NIH-funded researchers, they are the constituency that ultimately stands to gain the most from the policy's implementation. It is worth remembering the benefits that will emerge once the policy is in place.

Public access to NIH-funded research will not only greatly improve individual researchers' access to the work of their NIH-funded colleagues, but it will also vastly improve the exposure of NIH-funded works to a much wider community —increasing the reach, use, and ultimately, impact of their research.

The policy also enhances a researcher's ability to use and apply these articles in new and innovative ways. The PubMed Central database will be linked to the rich array of electronic resources already available from NIH—including GenBank, PubChem and, of course, PubMed—opening up new avenues for the conduct of research.

While it might feel initially to researchers that the requirement to retain appropriate rights is an extra burden, in the long run, it helps to promote awareness of the downstream effects that a choice of publishing venues can have on the reach and utility of their work. Understanding the power of effective copyright management strengthens the researchers' ability to ensure that their own work is read, used, and cited by the widest breadth of community they wish to see it.

## *ROLES FOR ADMINISTRATORS AND LEGAL COUNSEL*

Individual researchers may initially appear to shoulder the lion's share of the burden for complying with the NIH Public Access Policy, but ensuring compliance is actually a shared responsibility. If an institution receives NIH funds on behalf of their investigators, the institution is actually responsible for ensuring compliance with the policy. Recognizing the campus's responsibilities in this situation has opened up new roles for administrators on campus—particularly those responsible for research administration and legal oversight.

One critical role that research administrators can take is to ensure that NIH-funded investigators are aware of the new policy. While many campuses are already posting notices in electronic newsletters, sending out e-mail notifications, etc., others have seen success in posting standing notices in their online grants management systems, alerting researchers to the existence of the policy.[11]

Research administrators may also want to consider initiating educational sessions to help raise researcher awareness. Some campuses are finding that an effective combination is to hold a briefing session that involves: one or more research administrators, to outline the basics of what compliance entails; representatives from the library and/or institutional repository, to directly answer questions and offer assistance on compliance; and a legal expert, to answer questions and assist on working within the scope of rights retention issues. This approach is especially effective in illustrating the wider institution's commitment to facilitating compliance with this policy.

The area where the greatest uncertainty is bound to occur is in the rights arena. Administrators, particularly legal counsel or copyright officers, can play an active role in providing explicit assistance to researchers to ensure that appropriate rights are secured. This can mean helping authors to determine which journals have NIH policy-friendly copyright policies, helping researchers understand a publisher agreement they are about to sign, or providing researchers with institution-approved options for securing needed rights.

Options range from providing institution-specific, approved language to insert into the journal publications agreement of the endorsement of existing addenda, such as those offered by SPARC, Science Commons, and MIT.[12]

Given the increase in the number of public access policies being either implemented or considered, administrators and legal counsel may also wish to review current institutional policies on copyright and rights retention—to use this as an opportunity to reconfigure them and create a broad, systemic approach to facilitating compliance.

Finally, given the recognition that the liability for compliance ultimately rests with the institution, administrators may want to become actively involved in monitoring individual researchers' compliance with this policy. Options include using an online grants management system that can help track compliance or creating programs with libraries or repository managers who may also be able to provide automated mechanisms to facilitate this process.

## OPPORTUNITIES FOR ADMINISTRATORS AND LEGAL COUNSEL

The NIH Public Access Policy enhances the opportunity administrators and counsel have to contribute to a critical function of the university—ensuring that the institution remains an attractive place for agencies to direct funds. This policy can serve to open new channels between funding agency and university, perhaps encouraging even closer collaboration as both work to ensure compliance.

The NIH policy also affords administrators and legal counsel the chance to delve deeper into the scholarly communication process, to provide crucial support and insight in helping individual researchers to strengthen their ability to make educated decisions about the ultimate downstream reach and utility of their research outputs.

## ROLES FOR LIBRARIANS

The library community continues to play multiple, important roles in facilitating the success of the NIH Public Access policy. First and foremost, they can, and should, continue to actively advocate, locally and nationally, for the benefits that accrue to the entire academic community from the NIH and other public access policies. The implementation of the NIH policy by no means ensures its permanence, nor does it ensure that other agencies will now implement similar polices unimpeded by opposition. Active efforts by opponents to reverse this policy exist, and vocal support from the community remains crucial. It is important for the library community to continue to remind campus colleagues of the ultimate goals and benefits of the policy.

One way to encourage support for the current NIH policy and establish a solid foundation for future policies is for librarians to look for and publicize success stories on local campuses. Librarians can encourage researchers to share their positive experiences with the process and, especially, highlight new research mechanisms or results that emerge as a direct result of the availability of these articles in PubMed Central.

The NIH will continue to actively solicit input from the entire community on the policy and its implementation throughout the spring.

This is a great chance for the library community to participate and to share the best practices you see emerging at your institution that back the success of this policy.[13]

Libraries can also consider providing new services to assist researchers with the process of depositing papers into PubMed Central. Consider the possibility of working with repository managers to facilitate deposit. In particular, consider the possibilities that may exist to automate the process—perhaps by pushing articles directly from the repository into PubMed Central or enabling PubMed Central to sweep manuscripts from your repository.

Librarians have been effective, vocal advocates for author rights, and this policy offers a prime opportunity for the expansion of those educational campaigns. Consider programs that offer education and assistance to authors, whether they are workshops, webcasts, podcasts, etc.

The NIH policy is a great opening to work directly with your institution's legal counsel, not only to educate authors on how to comply, but also to advocate for new institutional policies on copyright and rights retention and access to research results. A white paper on campus advocacy for such policies is forthcoming from SPARC/Science Commons this spring.

## *OPPORTUNITIES FOR LIBRARIANS*

Given the recognition that facilitating compliance is actually a shared responsibility on campus, this policy provides a chance for the library community to create or deepen working relationships with colleagues in research administration and legal counsel positions.

The NIH Public Access Policy offers a rich opportunity for the library community to establish additional value-added services that are central to the workflows of faculty and researchers on campus, whether they are centered on deposit or rights management. These are issues that matter to the faculty, as they directly affect their research and ability to attract research funding. This, in turn, also provides a potential "calling-card" opportunity to engage faculty on a wider range of scholarly communications issues.

Once again, this policy places the library community in the center of the potential discussion for the establishment of new or enhanced institutional policies on access and rights management issues. It opens the door for the library to play a central role in the advocacy and development of such policies.

Finally, and perhaps most importantly, the NIH Public Access Policy provides the library with a direct opportunity to contribute to the advancement of the university's mission—the issue of efficient access to research being central to the role of higher education. A group of American university provosts expressed this succinctly in an Open Letter to the Higher Education Community in 2006: "The broad dissemination of the results of scholarly inquiry and discourse is essential for higher education to fulfill its long-standing commitment to the advancement and conveyance of knowledge. Indeed, it is mission critical."[14]

## NOTES

1. Consolidated Appropriations Act of 2008, http://thomas.loc.gov/cgi-bin/bdquery/z?d110:H.R.2764: (accessed July 6, 2008).
2. International Organization for Economic Cooperation and Development, "Report on Scientific Publishing," 2005, http://www.oecd.org/document/55/0,2340,en_2649_34487_35397879_1_1_1_1,00.html (accessed July 6, 2008).
3. National Institutes of Health Public Access Policy, http://publicaccess.nih.gov/policy.htm (accessed July 6, 2008).
4. SHERPA/ROMEO Database, University of Nottingham, http://www.sherpa.ac.uk/romeo.php (accessed July 7, 2008).
5. Carroll, Michael W., "Complying with the NIH Public Access Policy—Copyright Considerations and Options," *Joint SPARC/Science Commons publication*, http://www.arl.org/sparc/advocacy/nih/copyright.shtml (accessed July 7, 2008).
6. NIH Public Access Policy FAQ: http://publicaccess.nih.gov/FAQ.htm#c3.
7. Science, Commons, Scholar's Copyright Addendum Engine, http://scholars.sciencecommons.org/#form (accessed July 7, 2008).
8. NIH Manuscript Submission Website, http://publicaccess.nih.gov/ (accessed July 7, 2008).
9. List of Journals with current agreements with NIH, http://scholars.sciencecommons.org/#form (accessed July 7, 2008).
10. How to include PMCID in Citations, NIH Public Access Policy FAQ, http://publicaccess.nih.gov/FAQ.htm#c6 (accessed July 7, 2008).
11. Association of Research Libraries, "Institutional Responses to the NIH Public Access Policy," http://www.arl.org/sc/implement/nih/guide/response.shtml (accessed July 7, 2008).
12. Scholarly Publishing and Academic Resources Coalition, Author Rights Resources for Authors, http://www.arl.org/sparc/author/ (accessed July 7, 2008).
13. NIH Request for Information: The NIH Public Access Policy, http://publicaccess.nih.gov/comments.htm (accessed July 7, 2008).
14. 25 Universty Provosts, "*An Open Letter to the Higher Education Community*," Insider Higher Education, July 28, 2006, http://www.insidehighered.com/news/2006/07/28/provosts (accessed July 7, 2008).

# Deconstructing the Library: Reconceptualizing Collections, Spaces and Services

Sarah M. Pritchard

**ABSTRACT.** In the digital environment, we still have resources, staff, and facilities that combine in various ways to acquire and provide information. These recombinations challenge traditional definitions of library organization. Students and faculty now have many options for conducting their work, of which the traditional library is only one; the future of libraries—and librarians—will thus be in our ability to differentiate ourselves through unique and value added features. The library is not a single static entity, it is becoming a suite of services through which users locate, use, and (re)create research materials. By analyzing the intersection of factors such as subject, level of user, type of need, and proximity, we can develop a fine-tuned approach and customize services across the spectrum of physical, electronic, human, and material resources.

Regardless of the actual year and the specific trends, the professional literature and conferences are replete with writings about the emerging future and the trends in the external environments of education, technology, economic policy, publishing, and social behavior. Most of these are stimulating and thought provoking and prod us to think about the potential for our particular jobs and institutions.[1] At the same time, many things

---

Sarah M. Pritchard is Charles Deering McCormick University Librarian, Northwestern University, Evanston, IL.

in research libraries do not change much at all and we seem to muddle through. How do we identify the core mission and values of research libraries, while adapting to enormous and very real shifts in the methods and materials of academic information? We need to "deconstruct" the stereotypical categories of library resource and services, while sustaining the core concepts and models that still shape the nature of our profession. What we keep seeing in the digital environment is that our tools and locations are changing, but our goals and values are not.

When we describe the library's "role in the digital future," we are not talking simply about digital information, but about the transformation of the information environment that is happening as a result of digital technologies in our lives. This information environment still includes print and other physical forms of information; it still includes physical as well as virtual spaces, but these services, formats, and facilities are leveraged and extended, and new services and relationships are enabled through digital infrastructure. This has been an important theme of reports and articles in our field.[2] Digital infrastructure can be defined conceptually to include the spectrum created by interlinked digital content, digitally based business operations, digital communication and dissemination, digital research tools for analyzing and visualizing information, and digitally created "surrogate worlds" of which we are just seeing the early stages, things like Second Life or even in this view, MySpace since it has generated an entire social environment. What is exciting yet challenging about this infrastructure is that it undergirds even very traditional information objects and services such that librarians must engage in very holistic systems thinking as we organize and deliver services, allocate resources, and fulfill the goals for which a given library was established. All parts of a library are involved, not just some pieces that we can conveniently segregate as a special type of content or a special service.

At the same time, it is clear that the fundamental goals of library services have not changed. Libraries, librarians, and library services, broadly defined, are mechanisms to match people with information. Over the centuries we have made many choices about exactly how to do that matching, using cards, computers, or consultations, being active or passive, being selective or storing up everything just in case. A formal library, however, is today but one of the channels and mechanisms by which these two sides of the equation "find" each other, so we need to define ourselves more as a research information service of which one part might be an organized library. A successful research information service must reflect a dynamic understanding of the changes in three parallel structures:

1. the user community (in this case, the faculty and students, trustees and other stakeholders in higher education institutions)
2. the content (the creators and the publishing and media industries)
3. the interface (organizing systems, technology, direct services and facilities).

In the library and information world, we must constantly keep in mind the changing characteristics of the two external components of this equation, but it is especially the third part, the interface that enables the meshing of people and information, that typifies the work we do. Libraries, whether personal or institutional, are organized systems. If we look at the history of forms of classification, the urge to develop such systems goes back hundreds of years. The assumption seems to be implied that a given system will be able to encompass all present knowledge and be logically expandable to future topics. The store of information for which one needed the system could be brought together and expanded and remain stable in its order, even while growing. Even though new systems were developed periodically, each one was in itself a fixed pattern or approach (a few new numbers or shelves added within an existing system does not imply fundamental change). Therefore, the library as an interface was a set of physical and intellectual systems set up to await the users, one massive and passive array of information.

The digital environment, however, has transformed the passive sense of a building with books, which was in effect an information monopoly over which the user had little control, into an environment where the user has numerous choices, and the librarians themselves have numerous choices as to how to procure, deliver, and archive information. A single fixed system, either physical or bibliographic, will not work in the face of the flood of available content; moreover, users expect to be able to interact in a dynamic way with information, creating and reshaping the information and the organizing systems as their needs and mental models evolve. The breakthrough in the library's monopoly has been with the success and ubiquity of the end-user, point-of-service, and digital access to large quantities of relevant information. While users still need ways to get this information and they do prefer it organized, there are countless means of access that substitute for and bypass traditional libraries. Even if librarians are convinced that we have a better way, that message may get lost amidst the cacophony of all the competing messages, and the library just does not seem necessary to some users.

## DECONSTRUCTING AND REDEFINING "LIBRARY"

How can the library compete in this environment that is changing so rapidly when we have such a large number of conflicting demands, and we do not have the resources available to large commercial enterprises? How do we decide what to do amidst this plethora of choices? We still have a messy patchwork of different kinds of collections, facilities, technologies, and staff skills, as well as a diverse array of faculty and student demands and levels of institutional readiness. Despite articles encouraging a total redesign of the entire library operation, what might be called "blow it up and start over," most of us find this impractical for reasons of time, money, and politics. You can, however, redefine and "explode" the way you use the resources that you have at hand. We have great familiarity with our users, specifically, the advantage of being close to them physically and organizationally in academia, and we have institutional memory, and most important, credibility. The key is in reorienting our work to a much more refined definition of services, focusing on unique strengths, local needs, and multiple ways of delivering information. There are two trends in digital information that paradoxically converge, and these are the concepts of global and local. The global mass stores of digitized information are crucial and are expanding; their very size and ubiquity is what frees libraries locally to develop customized service directly aimed at our own institutions. This concept also underlies analyses by Betsy Wilson (this volume), Carla Stoffle, and Kim Leeder.[3]

We're all comfortable with recognizing that with digital technologies, the library is an "any time, any place" concept; the library can be defined as an abstract space, not a place. The word library, then, needs to be deconstructed. It conveys too much of a single definition of a collection in a building, designed to work in one linear way. The word barely even conveys the notion of people or services; we all have the feeling of invisibility that comes as some faculty swear that the "library" is the heart of the campus but when pressed, they rise not to protect the personnel budget but that for materials. Let's move to using library as a verb, not a noun, as a way of making more visible the level of activity that must happen in order to deliver those materials to the users.

I want thus to frame the research library as a suite of services designed to meet a range of needs. Collections, technologies, processing and public services—even the library building—are all forms of services that can be customized and deployed in different combinations to meet a much greater variety of needs than is the case when we view these things as undifferentiated wholes. Everything should now be (de)constructed and reassembled as an active, planned service, rather than a passive resource that functions according to one predetermined system, like a fixed reference desk open for set hours in one place with one level of consultation provided. Librarians and library staff must be the focus, not the overly vague word "library," because it is the people who are designing and providing the services that are now the key. They can mediate among the many resources, local and remote; they can set up facilities and technologies as appropriate; they can consult and advise on options for information management; they can design the interfaces that deliver the information or the service wherever the user is and in the ways most effective for the subject, the level of user, and the task at hand. This concept works even if we are simply placing physical books on shelves and letting people browse in the stacks. That is a specific choice that meets one particular need, but it is now obvious that it is only one of the many ways to characterize user needs and to deliver information services.

## *MISSIONS*

It sounds like a worn platitude to say that it is essential to define the mission of the library, but if we do it well, and I do not think we always do, then we gain significant shared understanding with our own stakeholders as to what we do and thus how we are prioritizing our resources. Embedded in that mission statement can be signals that place the concept of services to users at the front while still valuing the assembling of large collections that is the hallmark of research libraries. Research libraries are especially challenged since we do intend to keep materials we acquire from all over the world in many subjects and formats for very long periods of time, and we do not want to get rid of the back forty acres of stuff when we need to make room, physically or financially, for new services and publications. Serving the faculty and students of the university has been the conventional way to frame the mission statement, and that itself does imply quite differing levels and types of collections and services. If we also make explicit commitments in our mission to the preservation of important cultural heritage resources and the stewardship of the university's digital academic assets, then we have outlined two areas currently of great importance to research libraries that imply specific services and ways of allocating library resources like space, technology, and staff.

Research libraries have been the gatherers and protectors of nationally and internationally significant cultural heritage resources from the beginning. Too often, however, we are not clear about the implications of this for our institution's own goals. This can present a challenge in the higher education environment, though not so much at independent research libraries. Once a library has built an important and distinctive collection of the kind generally described as a "special collection," we have made an implied commitment to the rest of our peer research libraries that we are going to sustain and enhance that collection. Special collections are expensive to acquire, process, house, and preserve, and few libraries are going to start from scratch in an area if they know another library already has exhaustive research level holdings. This may mean spending scarce resources in an area that, in any given semester, could be irrelevant to the needs of the specific faculty and students right there at that time. This can be a risky thing to admit in some public institutions where the legislature may be focused on a very short-term definition of outcomes, and they do not want to invest any more than what is needed to support the research and curriculum being pursued that year. We should show that it is a source of institutional pride and competitiveness to have resources of this kind, and we can appeal to the institution's sense of supporting the greater social good, but we should be honest about the costs. Most libraries can readily itemize the special collections to which they have strong ongoing commitments, and it is not a long list compared to the overall scope of the library. These collections are ones for which we could legitimately say that they are ends in themselves. As I will make clearer a little later, this has direct bearing on how we deconstruct the nature of collections and then focus on more customized services.

The second area in which mission statements can help clarify the scope of library operations and support new roles is that of the stewardship of our parent institution's digital academic assets. This is an extension of the role of university archives that many research libraries already fulfill. In the digital environment, however, it opens up roles for librarians in several domains either not dealt with at all or handled in an eclectic and uncoordinated fashion. The long-term curation of university business records in digital form is woefully under-implemented at most institutions including my own. To say there are backups made at the level of the computer system files is not the same as a persistent and retrievable digital archive as we now define those. This is an opportunity to position the library as an active partner with campus IT and administrative operations offices to develop the archiving systems and the data and metadata structures necessary, but as logical as it may seem, it still presents fractious political difficulties. It requires a deconstructing of the word library and even of the word archive to piece apart the specific information services that can be brought to bear at the institutional level and that librarians are often uniquely qualified to provide. Stewardship of digital academic assets extends to institutional repositories for faculty publishing, grey literature, courseware, back files of commercial digital publications, and the library's own digital productions. Defining these together as institutional assets presents a business model in which information services are critical to the long-term history, competitiveness, and sustainability of the university. Such services go beyond traditional definitions of library collections or facilities; thus it is advisable to have this role defined in a mission statement.

## USERS

The examples described above in the context of mission statements amount to defining new groups of users that can be primary targets for library services, such as external cultural heritage organizations, university administrators, public stakeholders, and even unidentified future researchers. These are not truly new users or new audiences, but they are users that we can do more to highlight and for whom our services can be highly relevant. They are not the main or the only user group, so it is essential to have a way to balance library resources. To recast its work as a suite of services, expanding and customizing while also sustaining certain traditional operations, a library can develop a detailed matrix of user characteristics that helps identify the information resources and delivery methods appropriate to each group. There are at least three dimensions to this "faceted classification" of users: the subject area of the information need; the level of the user (e.g., lower division undergraduates, grad students, junior faculty, clinical researchers); the task at hand (quick facts, in-depth research, scholarly publishing, integrating media in the classroom). The location of the user also helps define the options for specific services as might individual factors, such as accessibility or language.

These characteristics should not surprise anyone; librarians have always looked at users in these ways as we have developed collections and facilities. What may be different in the digital environment is the greater ease in developing niche or tailored services. Because the majority of current core collections are increasingly digital, and most users prefer this format for their routine research and educational purposes, we can focus on the fringe areas where the materials are not digital or require specialized interventions, or we can launch new services such as publishing or the archiving of digital scientific data. When I refer to a niche service, the assumption is that not every person needs every service, and therefore, libraries can offer some services that if they were widely adopted, might be prohibitively expensive or logistically impractical. This can also help make up for the loss of traditional services to which longtime faculty have become accustomed, for example, the delivery of books from the campus library to faculty offices if they place a request through the OPAC. This is not a new idea but lots of libraries still do not do it because mail delivery staff object, the campus is too large to have a student assistant truck things around, or it is thought that the workload will be too great. Well, the number of faculty who need large numbers of newly identified print monographs every single day is dwindling steadily. For those who still work this way, primarily faculty using older materials in the humanities and the humanistic social sciences, the delight of getting all the books they flagged in the library catalog without having to leave their office, promotes better satisfaction with the library and may even help overcome resistance to the shift of hundreds of thousands of volumes to secondary storage. This demonstrates the ways in which the digital environment enables more services even when it is a traditional service; the transactions from the faculty office are part of the digital communications and cataloging systems, and the fact that the delivery of hard copy is now more manageable is because the larger proportion of daily information browsing is taken care of by digital information resources.

Within the cells of the matrix delineating subjects, levels, and tasks of library users, we have effectively deconstructed the notion of an undifferentiated user, and library staff can analyze how best to apportion resources across the needs and preferences revealed in this way. "Resources" include varying formats of collections, of course, as well as technologies, delivery mechanisms, reproduction services, staff expertise, buildings and facilities, and resources to which we have access through campus or consortial collaborations.

## *SERVICES AND SKILLS*

Libraries have become more and more service oriented over the past century, though this was not always the mode of a research library and in some countries today it still is not. If you did not know how to use it, you did not belong there, and the work of digging out the information was the test of the mettle of a scholar. Even if a redefinition of a library as a suite of services seems a self-evident nonissue to many newer in the profession, it cannot be taken for granted that library operations actually are based on this notion or that library staff see their work in this way. A core library service used to be a library's own stacks, or its own databases, or even its own Web site, but those have been exploded or supplanted by the availability of easy external choices for seeking information. The OPAC and the ILS are not controlling or even comprehensive anymore.

Library services present a spectrum of approaches to acquiring, managing, evaluating, synthesizing, delivering, and preserving information; usually this is seen as a centralized or institutional approach, managing the resources owned by the enterprise. We can now add to that a parallel role as information consultants, working with users to help them manage, use and preserve the personal research information they accumulate and generate in their professional work. Librarians' skills can be decoupled, not only from the physical library as their place of work, but also from the collection of items owned by the library. Information management skills are increasingly central to universities at every level, and librarians are poised to deploy them in an exciting variety of settings.

To match information resources and services to users we need to rethink and deconstruct the nature of the collection, the nature of the delivery mechanisms used to move collections and information tools to users, and the staff skills needed for given combinations of those. The group of things that we have lumped together as public services, for example, can be split from their traditional moorings at the desk. Even the split between the departments is blurred as many staff work across those functions. As libraries try to locate new services within typical organization charts, where does one put things like digital publishing, scholarly communication support, or information management consultation, in which we advise faculty about structure and metadata for their own databases and Web sites? These are increasingly important services, yet formalizing them requires taking apart older notions of departments and tasks. Staff expertise helps define an organizational structure that is more focused on services. This has been true in the past with collections' units organized around specific subjects or languages, but the difference I am suggesting is that the person, the physical location, and the collections or technologies can each be treated—conceptually, at least—as independent sets of resources to be recombined as needed.

Reference is no longer place-specific as it can be happening through online chat and IM; what does this mean for where the actual librarians can be located in the meantime? Information literacy instruction can be delivered in person, via the Web, or now through podcasts. Library staff with the right technical knowledge can be providing metadata, digitizing, archiving, and related programming work regardless of whether this is in support of the library's in-house needs, faculty research, or other institutional projects. Instead of itemizing a list of trendy innovative library services, I want to outline how new concepts of collections and of delivery are defining factors in reshaping those services.

## DELIVERING RESOURCES

The notion of delivery is common in libraries and is usually taken to refer to bookmobiles, interlibrary loan mailings, shuttles between branch locations, and now, digital transmission. Modes of delivering services can be construed more broadly, and it is that broadening that allows a more strategic deployment of resources and almost a modular component approach to designing services to meet specific niches of user needs. In addition to vehicles, mail, and telecommunications, people are a form of delivery, and most interestingly, so are buildings. Buildings, and within them types of rooms, are another way to deliver the services needed by some users. Building-centric delivery is ideal for users that want consultation or group study, want to use rare materials, or do research that integrates the rare and the digital. Central campus library buildings are perfect for people oriented uses, for high-use resources or valuable materials, for collections that require expertise close at hand, and for special technologies that are not widely available. But with the scarcity of campus space and the expense of research library facilities, do we really need to use the main building as the delivery mechanism for all of the general collections? We can move lesser used, nonrare materials and items for which there are digital surrogates to secondary storage while renovating core library spaces to be much more customized for specific types of users, staff and collections. Both faculty and students still want to be in the library buildings but for quite different purposes; by deconstructing the idea of the building as a massive entity, and by viewing it now as one of many choices for delivery, maybe we can stop talking just about "the library" and more about "library services" and, even better, "librarians."

The role of librarians and library staff as themselves being methods of delivery is not something new, but it has taken a long time to get the notion out of people's heads that the library is a specific place with physical assets, and you have to go there to get things done and the staff are a pleasant afterthought, if you think about them at all. It is that outdated but persistent notion that leads even sophisticated faculty to say things like "I never use the library anymore, I just go online," or that leads those faculty to vote to protect the collections budgets from cuts while allowing, directly or indirectly, reductions in staff that prevent the very acquisitions and systems design and other services needed to bring them the collections they defended. By putting librarians out there as faculty services specialists, we promote their role as academic partners and we advance the concept that "building" and "collections" are only parts of the array of information services that we can deliver. In some subjects where the traditional collections may be weak or still emerging, the librarian is increasingly the "glue" that helps users by advising on local and remote collections, print and digital, cooperative resource sharing, vendor services, scholarly publishing, and things like reserves, instruction, and course management support. To see the librarians as these independent sources of expertise, they have to get out from behind desks and even out of the physical building. The embedded librarian has long been common in libraries that support corporate projects and research facilities, and we are starting to see them in university settings. These are librarians that hold office hours (or are even permanently based) in the academic departments for which they are liaisons or that staff small service outposts in residence halls or student services buildings. They are near their collections only in the virtual sense; more importantly, they are near their users.

For some subjects and some users, all that is needed is digital delivery. The content, regardless of the owning repository, the consultation through email or live chat, the transactions for archiving, lending, or copying, the tools for authoring and repackaging, and more are all available at the keyboard. This truly decouples the user, the collection, and the facilities and fosters very direct access. It can be so successful that the user is unaware of how much design, programming, and funding went into ensuring that those resources landed on their laptop. There can be clever ways to approach branding screens and nesting Web sites to remind users of a library presence, or maybe we should not worry about the potential for invisibility and just find ways to build in user feedback tools that will help the behind-the-scenes library make the case at budget time.

There is one other form of delivery that is quite common yet not viewed in this context; collaboration. Libraries are excellent at developing collaborative relationships with all sorts of partners across campus, with teaching and technology groups, regionally with other libraries, and nationally with publishers, vendors, and professional and educational organizations. In this sense of delivery, some other organization is getting the actual content or service out to the user, but it is through the network of organized collaboration that it is enabled. It is easy to add "collaboration" as another mechanism by which libraries match users with content, and it should be better integrated into our overall planning for how to customize and expand services for particular needs. If we are deconstructing the library, then the result is that we cannot view it as a stand-alone entity. Because there are so many channels for users to get information, in effect, we want to seek out those very channels and collaborate with them to enhance the overall value added for users and for the role of librarians. A prime example of this notion is the number of libraries flocking to work out deals with Google and Microsoft for digitizing, search linking tools, data management, and more. If you cannot beat them, join them. What's great is that they still need libraries in order to get hold of real content, which brings me to the deconstruction of collections.

## COLLECTIONS

Collections are not a goal in themselves, even in research libraries. Collections, whether print or digital, are a service, a way of matching information content with the people who seek it, and thus can be built and delivered in different ways depending on the type of information needed and the type of user of the service. This is a difficult shift for some librarians, who have had the luxury of exclusively collection-focused work, to accept. Even though the traditional bibliographer is generally following the priorities of the academic program, in research libraries this linkage can get rather distant. The bibliographer, a word I use purposely for its connotation of an older model, gets into a mesmerizing self-referential inward spiral building for the perfection of the collection as judged against some abstract standard that, even in the more elaborate collection development policies, does not always articulate a concept of users or institutional stakeholders.

Collection management, in the digital environment (by which I do not necessarily mean only digital collections), can be deconstructed into three distinctive areas of work that can each be the focus of an operational service area. First, despite the assertion I just made, some collections are an end in themselves; those are the well-defined "special collections" that are the hallmark of research libraries. These will in fact be even more important as a way to differentiate the strengths of various libraries. As more and more libraries subscribe to the same large commercial packages of digital content, the average undergraduate student is going to get the same collection of information everywhere. What will vary is the research level collections, and in addition to the typical special collections, this will include distinctive aggregations of more general materials defined by a subject or language focus. Each library will likely maintain and refine its definitions of what it considers its commitments to special collections because of the expense and time commitment these imply. By definition, they cannot be purchased or cataloged consortially; they may not be part of vendor-provided packages; they may require local cataloging from scratch, customized piece by piece digitizing and preservation and extra security. The special collections are the parts of a research library being built for the greater good of the worldwide network of cultural heritage organizations and often for an unknown future user.

What has been defined as the "general collections" will be increasingly developed through massive digital stores paired with secondary storage, just-in-time digital delivery, and interlibrary lending, as is already somewhat the case. This body of information resources must be acquired and delivered to meet the needs of the current faculty and students. Librarians need to view collection development work as one of a set of services they deliver to faculty along with support for course-specific instructional sessions, reserves, media, consultation about scholarly communication, data archiving, and the other things I mentioned earlier. Faculty are too absorbed in their own work to be expected to remember all sorts of names and locations for who does what in the library, and the people they trust are the ones that understand their field. We need to work on their terms and not expect them to fit our models. The subject librarian can function as the liaison for any information service needed, working with the department faculty as an academic partner and later making the arrangements with the relevant units behind the scenes at the library. In effect, this is a public services and outreach function where the faculty and upper division students and graduate students are the targeted groups.

The third facet of collection management, as I'm deconstructing it, is defined by a group of services and vendor relationships that has become increasingly technically complex. Except for special collections, acquisitions has become more a function of elaborate aggregated packages, approval plans, consortial contracts, and content bundled with metadata and end-processing services. Selection of items on a one by one basis is just not how we are building large general collections, and therefore, it should be managed as a technical and business operation and not as part of the subject-specific liaison function. Furthermore, the electronic resource management systems needed to track these packages and contracts, the specific titles and subjects covered by each, and the licensing provisions and allowable uses are a specialized support function that must integrate with other inventory control, cataloging, and vendor ordering systems.

In this model, collection development has been redefined as a combination of three areas: general collections—which become a public services/liaison function; technical acquisitions and resource management; and special collections.

## *REMAPPING THE DOMAIN*

It is a bit of a contrivance to use the concept of "deconstruction" in this study of organizational strategy because it is not really a direct extension of the meaning that the term has in literary theory. It does turn out, however, that even the literary theorists cannot give a simple definition of what deconstruction stands for. As an analytical model, however, it forces us to think on several levels including taking something apart that had been previously built or taking elements from within the "text"—which one might say is the library as a living narrative—and using them to undercut the purported meaning of the whole. Library leaders and staff need to do this deconstruction so that stagnation does not set in, and we can incorporate new services and collections while still living within the same budgets and buildings. Right now, this is especially critical because of the speed with which the digital environment has permeated our entire world and, as I have been emphasizing, because of the many ways our intended audiences may now find research information without entering a formal library. We need to flip things over and look at them from a different angle. There are other metaphors that can accomplish this, one of which might be cartographic: this is a remapping of both the conceptual and physical domains called "the library." Cartography, or perhaps holography, could be what we need to get a three-dimensional map of the intersection of types of users, different subject needs, and physical and virtual forms of delivery; at each node of intersection we can craft a service, and it is that matrix array, that suite, which is the library.

## NOTES

1. Strategic planning frameworks for libraries stress these factors, such as the ACRL Research Committee, *Environmental Scan 2007* (Chicago: Association of College and Research Libraries, 2007), http://ala.org/ala/acrl/acrlpubs/whitepapers/Environmental_Scan_2.pdf (accessed March 1, 2008); and the *SOLINET Member Scenario Planning Discussions* held April 23, 2007 (Atlanta, GA: Southeastern Library Network, Inc., 2007), http://www.solinet.net/emplibfile/scenarioplanningreport.pdf (accessed March 1, 2008).

2. See for example Campbell, Jerry D., "Changing a Cultural Icon: The Academic Library as a Virtual Destination," *EDUCAUSE Review* 41, no. 1 (January/February 2006): 16–31; and Lougee, Wendy Pradt, *Diffuse Libraries: Emergent Roles for the Research Library in the Digital Age* (Washington, DC: Council on Library and Information Resoures, August 2002).

3. Stoffle, Carla J. and Kim Leeder. "Where Next? Library Transformation," presented at *Living the Future 6*, April 5–8, 2006, Tucson, AZ, http://www.library.arizona.edu/conferences/ltf/2006/documents/LTF_transformation.ppt (accessed March 1, 2008).

# Out of the Gray Times: Leading Libraries into the Digital Future

Deborah Jakubs

**ABSTRACT.** Past practices, policies, and staffing patterns have served as a solid foundation for research libraries. New challenges require a fresh—and very different—look at much of what we have taken for granted over decades. This presentation will discuss the changes in philosophy, organizational models, and recruitment that are needed to reposition libraries for the digital future.

Two decades ago, when my older son was just about four years old and still an only child, one of his favorite pastimes was to watch reruns of the original "Lassie" shows. We often watched together, immersed in the adventures of Timmy and his brave dog, familiar to me from my own childhood. The sense of continuity was comforting, a link from the present to the past, another connection between us.

One evening, out of the blue, he asked, "Mommy, were you and Daddy alive in the gray times?" At first I did not grasp his meaning, but then it dawned on me: Lassie and Timmy lived in the gray times, and we lived in the Technicolor times. Black-and-white TV shows portrayed the gray times, before the world changed and became much more complicated, varied, and beautiful. A lot like Kansas before Oz, or maybe Pleasantville.

---

Deborah Jakubs is Rita DiGiallonardo Holloway University Librarian, Vice Provost for Library Affairs, Duke University, Durham, NC.

I have carried this memory with me for the obvious reasons related to family (it is a favorite story), but lately I have also begun to see it as a metaphor for the work and lives of libraries (and librarians) as we face and embrace the digital future. We did, in fact, live and work in the "gray times," though we did not know it; we were satisfied, comfortable, and even happy. The challenges were predictable, and we understood the world and our role in it. People came to us for help, and we provided that authoritative assistance. Our help was of critical importance to their success. We anticipated their needs and provided services to meet those needs, from collection development to cataloging, from inter-library loan to reference desks.

I mean no disrespect by saying we lived in the gray times; it was the world we all knew and understood and in which we thrived. Now, however, we have stepped out of that world. Indeed, we are already living in the digital future in which users of libraries have many other options when it comes to seeking information, in which we know much less what to expect, in which our patrons are becoming experts themselves. This has been stimulating and unsettling at the same time. It has left some librarians wondering about the value of all they have contributed over their careers. It is incumbent on us to facilitate this transition, to position our libraries and prepare our staff for the rapid changes of the digital present and the digital future, as far ahead as we can see. We must be careful, at the same time, to respect the legacy of the gray times.

The role of the research library, it is no secret, has become more complex. Library buildings and the purposes for which they are being designed and utilized have changed dramatically. Relationships between library staff and the user communities (on-site as well as remote) have expanded, and their interactions have grown more sophisticated. Librarians are developing new facility with technologies and are engaged in new, closer ways with researchers. Formerly places in which primarily to engage in quiet reading and contemplation or from which to retrieve materials to take away and use, our research libraries are now twenty-four-hour beehives of group work, social interactions, and the creation of innovative scholarship that spans formats. The expanded role of the library, and of librarians, means we must anticipate, and reach to provide, the most advanced technological access to a wide array of digital resources without losing sight of our most basic commitment to the preservation of scholarship in print form. Our special collections have come to distinguish one research library from another as our online collections become more and more similar through licensed access to e-resources by the thousands. Creating better access to the old, establishing new links to all materials that support scholarship, and extending the reach of our special collections are important ways we are heading into the digital future.

## CREATING INTELLECTUAL COMMUNITY

The reinvigoration of libraries has come as a surprise to many, including university administrators and the general public, who have questioned whether there is even a need for the physical library given the availability of digital resources. Not only is there a need, but it is even more compelling as the range of activities the library supports grows wider. As a Duke first-year student remarked, "The library is where intellectual communities are formed," explaining the late night scene in the reading rooms in which students learn from one another about courses they are taking, projects in which they are engaged, and ideas they are pursuing; it is obvious that learning is increasingly informal, complementing the formal. Another student commented that she goes to the library "when I want to get serious." It *is* possible to study in one's dorm room, but students do not generally do so. This is due to the "push" factors—noise, interruptions, the discomfort of spending even more time in such a small space—as well as the "pull" factors— inspiring environment, access to scholarly resources, comfortable and varied seating options, a coffeehouse, and a socially stimulating setting—of the modern library.

Student demand for longer hours has led us to keep the libraries open twenty-four hours most days of the week. The library has become that "third place," described in *The Great Good Place*, where people can gather simply for the pleasures of good company and lively conversation, putting aside the concerns of work and home.[1] Similarly cited in *Pattern Recognition*, this is the place "whose mission is defined by service, where people can work unobserved and can develop as they wish."[2] This vitality and our newfound popularity, bring us pleasure and pride, as we see how central the library is to the social and intellectual lives of our students. The role also requires some adjustments: expanded staffing (Duke now has reference librarians on duty until 2:00 AM in our two principal libraries); additional security and housekeeping services; enhanced user spaces, often at the expense of on-site physical collections; and relaxed food and drink policies, given that students are now practically living in the library during certain times of the semester.

Just as library users seek different kinds of study and research spaces, they also expect new library services. Those expectations are predicated on having immediate and round-the-clock access to information, books, e-reserves, answers to questions, and online delivery of articles. Once, not that long ago, e-mail reference service was a great innovation; now it is too slow for students and has been replaced by chat, instant messaging, and virtual reference service. At Duke, in just two years, chat reference questions increased by 212 percent, IM questions by 256 percent, and virtual reference (Tutor.com and Velaro) questions by 155 percent. The trend continues upward. At the same time, from 2005 to 2007, reference transactions at the desk saw a small overall decline while the number of content and extended questions rose somewhat. We know that users have a choice of where to get information, and libraries still seek to be among the first, most reliable, and trusted locations to satisfy those needs, whether in person or virtually.

In the gray times, libraries boasted excellent public service, but in developing those services, paid relatively little attention to what users wanted, what users preferred, and how users did their work. Today, in comparison, we have very savvy users who come to us with more sophisticated questions, abilities, and suggestions and higher expectations. Librarians feel the pressures and potential of these heightened expectations, along with the hot breath of the Googles of the world with which our services often compete. We must adapt and innovate and stay at least a step ahead of our users if we are not just to survive, but to thrive.

## *FLEXIBLE, NIMBLE, RESPONSIVE*

Research libraries have always taken their cues from the universities of which they are a part, responding to new program development, curricular changes, and shifts in the directions of research. As the digital landscape becomes more complex and the range of resources needed to support teaching and research expands, libraries must continue to prove their value to the university and demonstrate that the very significant investment made in the library is well directed and well spent, an investment not only in our buildings, staff, and collections, but also in the academic success of students and faculty. As new technologies are integrated into the academic realm, libraries must be flexible, nimble, and responsive. The challenge of maintaining both print and digital collections is mirrored in the need to provide technology services and support to a wider spectrum of users, from the researcher still firmly grounded in the gray times to the most innovative scientist.

As the increased use of the physical spaces and the undeniable value of the diverse services we provide become more obvious to the university administration, it is a time of great opportunity for the library. This can lead to an even more central role for the library. At Duke, for example, a new library addition that essentially doubled our space opened in fall 2005, and our popularity as a destination for students skyrocketed. The administration could not help but take note (there was a 40 percent increase in the number of people coming to the libraries, a 25 percent increase in print circulation, and we are now a hot stop on the regular tours for prospective new students), and soon we were engaged in collaborative planning with the provost, the deans, the chief information technology officer, and faculty to renovate what was to have become technical services space on the lower floor and convert it to a Teaching and Learning Center (TLC) offering classrooms, breakout rooms, and other creative spaces, all well equipped with technology tools. Thus the libraries will facilitate the full spectrum of learning, from informal to formal, professor to student, student to student, and librarian to student, inside and outside the classroom. We will also put in place an integrated, highly collaborative, "all things technology" staffing model among the libraries, the Office of Information Technology, and Arts & Sciences. The evolution of the TLC is an excellent example of adapting our plans as we see how the building is being used, learning from our patrons. To some, the idea of turning library space into classrooms might seem like a slippery slope, giving away to "them" something that is "ours;" I see it as an exceptional opportunity to partner with other units on campus and to prove once again the renewed centrality of the libraries to the academic enterprise.

## *THE CHALLENGE OF INTERDISCIPLINARITY*

Like many other universities, Duke has placed a renewed emphasis on interdisciplinary scholarship. Far from the old model of a team-taught course that featured two professors from different departments, the new interdisciplinarity has many versions. Cross-school faculty appointments, the creation of new institutes, e.g., for global health, brain sciences, or visual studies, and boundary-crossing from the humanities to the sciences—all are examples of this new dynamic, which also frequently engages faculty from other universities, often beyond the United States, in collaborative research projects. What does this mean for research libraries? In the gray times, we organized our staff and our budgets around disciplinary divisions, with bibliographers or liaisons for this or that department, carrying out collection development and monitoring the materials budget for their respective fields, attending academic department meetings, serving as conduits for information moving in both directions—department-library and library-department. Now, we are challenged to provide new kinds of services that target the research and teaching that is not restricted to a single discipline. Team-based program liaisons—including librarians from the professional schools, librarian links to a customized set of resources on course Web sites, and more flexible budgeting—are all among the strategies required to meet this new challenge. We are also called on to produce reports that combine data from multiple areas and across schools to demonstrate how a given interdisciplinary program is supported by the library. Adding to the complexity is the need to assess the relevance and impact of those many databases that cross traditional disciplinary lines. In the gray times, we could easily say what the library spent on sociology, art, or biology—but those strictly disciplinary divisions are losing relevance.

In response to a more interdisciplinary focus, the libraries at Duke are making several changes. Facing the renovation of the building in which the chemistry library was located, and given the very slim possibility of seeing the construction of a new consolidated sciences library, we made the decision (in consultation with a faculty committee) to integrate the library into our main (now expanded) library. Thus, chemistry, its staff, and part of its collections became part of the main library in 2007. Over the next two years, we will add two other branch libraries for math, physics, computer science and engineering, and the biological and environmental sciences. We will merge the staff of these branches with central staff and look forward to the consolidation of a truly interdisciplinary library with highly responsive and robust services to all users. The Provost fully approves of this direction, and has provided not only moral support but also significant funding ($3.5 million) to acquire thousands of e-journal back files so we can move all the physical volumes offsite rather than into the main library. Naturally, faculty and students are very pleased to have this enhanced digital access to the journal literature and find the newer main library spaces to be more inviting and conducive to group work than the much older branch spaces. We expect to retain several (bookless) library "satellites" among the science buildings as reading rooms and study spaces featuring librarian office hours and delivery points for materials from our offsite stack facility as well as interlibrary loan.

Much interdisciplinary work relies on data and GIS. Another important change we have made is to create a Data Services unit to provide expertise to the campus. Several academic departments, including economics and the School of the Environment, have partnered with the libraries and are providing graduate student assistants who complement the work of the professional librarians who staff Data Services. As more seniors at Duke opt to submit an honors thesis (the number has risen from 16 percent of the senior class to over 30 percent), we are seeing much more use of primary data among undergraduates. This new unit will respond well to that need.

## CHALLENGES ARE OPPORTUNITIES

The heightened expectations of users and interest among our administrators in ensuring that our libraries can meet those expectations compel us to engage in fresh thinking about how we are organized, what skills we seek in new hires, and what leadership we provide. Of course it is not possible to begin completely anew and construct the "dream team," but it can be a provocative basis for productive discussion to contemplate what staffing, service, and collections models we would devise if we were starting from scratch in this digital world.

First of all, we need to put energy into revising the image of the library and the people who work there to reflect the true nature, extent, and sophistication of the services offered. In short, we need to stop talking just to ourselves and market the library better. In the gray times, people sought us out because they needed us; we were the only game in town when it came to finding trustworthy information. Times have changed, and an information-rich society surrounds us. A traditional image no longer describes the research library accurately. Of course nothing spreads the word better than excellent service and satisfied library users, but we must be energetic and enthusiastic in promoting our collections and services.

Reorganizing, retraining, and rethinking what we do are among the most difficult yet potentially most rewarding challenges we face. For many staff, particularly those who have been working in libraries since the gray times, it can be a stressful transition. For example, as we incorporate more elements of Library 2.0, inviting users (wherever they may be) to contribute metadata to describe digital collections, or as we link to Wikipedia for quick access to information, or as we pursue new avenues of access to the information in our online catalogs, it may seem to some that the library's role as the authoritative, trusted source of good, solid, and accurate information is eroding dangerously and that we are even helping that process along. It is important, as leaders, to be sensitive to staff concerns and to convey an appreciation for the critical role they have played in establishing the foundations of today's library services. We could not have emerged from the gray times at all were it not for the dedication of our staff and their commitment to providing excellent services to our users.

That said, we must also encourage librarians and other staff to take on new roles and to see the benefits of enlarging their perspectives and experiences. Our people should be playing with the same technologies and tools that our students and other users are employing, becoming familiar with new approaches to research and information-seeking. staff should be expected to learn about new tools and new approaches to research and should be responsible for pursuing their continuing education. They should be encouraged to read widely and to pay attention to trends. The library can facilitate that learning through presentations, seminars, classes, conferences, and open discussions.

We must actively recruit new staff with the skills, creativity, and curiosity to enable the library to innovate and then set them loose to do so. Although a number of library schools are preparing students to take on these challenges, there are many roads to research library work. It behooves us to look broadly for new staff with the appropriate talents and not just the usual credentials. As Stanley Wilder has commented, "The need for new kinds of expertise has driven ARL libraries to hire a substantial and growing number of individuals with no library education."[3] This is due in large part to the more complex role of libraries, the expansion of services and programs, and the ubiquity of technology.

As Wilder goes on to discuss, these new functions have led us to look to different groups, people with skills in instructional technology, systems support, budgeting and assessment, digital archiving, etc. We need—and should welcome—them all. The issue is reminiscent of the 1990s focus on the future of area studies librarianship and the perceived shortage of specialists with the deep knowledge of regions and languages that would be required to support academic programs. Acknowledging that there may be multiple paths to library work, the Mellon Foundation established several programs to attract recent PhDs to the field, in area studies and the humanities. The implication that the MLS might not be an absolute requirement for professional librarian positions stimulated concern about the future of the MLS since non-MLS "librarians" were increasingly being hired into professional positions in research libraries. Concern was raised about a possible trend toward hiring "feral librarians."[4]

The word "feral" implies wild, untamed, and in need of domestication; rather than trying to "civilize" those individuals and to bring them to see the world as librarians do, we should take advantage of the chance to diversify our staff. More "feral" tendencies and different experiences can enrich our organizations. After all, even if these professionals do not have degrees in library science, presumably they have used libraries, whether for pleasure or for research. Their perspectives as sophisticated library users can help shape future library services. Paying more attention to the skills and less to the need for an absolute set of credentials will go far to bring about fundamental, beneficial changes in our libraries. This is, after all, another kind of diversity.

## *MIDDLE MANAGERS AS CHANGE AGENTS*

Our middle managers play a critical role in effecting change and in preparing staff for the digital future. This group has the responsibility both to advocate for their staff and their departments and to interpret and implement the strategies of the library leadership, two tasks that may seem at times to be in mutual conflict. Wilder's work on the "graying" of the profession stresses the urgency of recruiting the next generation of librarians. I believe that the key to transforming our organizations is to put in place middle managers who can envision the future and provide effective leadership while also working collaboratively across departments for the greater good of the organization. They should model the attitudes and behaviors that will enable our libraries to progress and our staff to face the future with a willingness to entertain and embrace new ideas. These managers should engage their staff in determining the future and bring the best ideas to the attention of the organization as a whole. They should be mentors too and ensure that their staff members have the professional development opportunities they need and deserve, whether they are taking on new responsibilities or acquiring new skills. They should help identify things we can stop doing and free staff to pursue departmental and institutional priorities. They—and we—should reward innovation and creativity, and curb fear of change by successfully articulating the purpose and value of a particular initiative or direction. These are key appointments in our organizations and central to efforts to lead our libraries into the digital future.

## OVERCOMING RESISTANCE

Librarians have the well-deserved reputation of being the experts, the authorities, and the interpreters. The digital world increasingly demands that we take our cues from users, learning as much as possible about how they do their work and then designing services that facilitate that work, anticipating their needs. This is the case especially with students, as each year's freshman class is more adept with technology than the previous. We also have more opportunities to collaborate with faculty and other researchers and to provide a different kind of expertise than we have in the past. The recent report from the Association of Research Libraries, *Agenda for Developing E-Science in Libraries*,[5] states, "E-science has the potential to be transformational within research libraries by impacting their operations, functions, and possibly even their mission...[T]rends in e-science...impact collections, services, research infrastructure, and professional development." It is imperative that we expose our library staff to the latest trends—this is not optional—and that we engage the organization in active planning to embrace these new opportunities for deeper, even more satisfying involvement in our universities. The possibilities are exciting and we should encourage our staff to direct their energy towards innovative programs and ways to showcase new services.

There may well be staff resistance to "lowering our standards," for example, in the great Wikipedia debate (to link or not to link), as we take our lead more and more from library users and shape our services according to what they want. There is nothing to be gained and much to be lost by stubbornly adhering to the position that only through the library can one find information of value. Rather than fearing and resisting the fact that users can now find useful information on their own, our libraries should be shoulder-to-shoulder with those very users, understanding how they do their work and where the library can add value to that work. We should assume a position of strength, not weakness. Rather than being defensive about "threats" to the traditional position of libraries, we should tout the advantages of the contemporary research library. There may be more than one information "game" in town, but ours has plenty to offer.

## FINDING THE FUNDING

Among the most pressing challenges of bringing the research library fully into the digital future is determining how to pay for it. This is a process that requires that we identify and weigh the trade-offs and determine what we can give up in order to take on new roles. The impact on the materials budget of acquiring both print and digital resources is old news now, not a relic of the gray times, but a familiar challenge. Rising costs of electronic journals and databases are well documented and have plagued us for some time. Now we face other new costs related to expanding our services. Keeping buildings open for twenty-four hours, for example, has budgetary implications, particularly for security, housekeeping and maintenance, student workers, and the replacement of computers and printers. Expanding e-reserves has meant that more is spent on staff in those units as well as on mundane items such as paper and toner cartridges. Providing to the campus the specialized expertise of scholarly communication experts and launching copyright education among faculty represent other relatively new library functions and important services to the university.

Actively marketing the full range of library services means that more resources are needed for communication, publicity, and maintaining connections with alumni and library donors. Surfacing our rich special collections through digital means and promoting their use, positioning the library to lead in the establishment and maintenance of digital repositories, and ensuring that library staff and services are connected to Blackboard sites and closely involved with other instructional technologies all require either new positions or the redeployment of vacant ones. Making sure that our staff has the conference travel opportunities, professional training, and retraining they need to participate fully in these exciting new roles also requires an investment. As we seek to hire larger numbers of talented new library staff, we face stiff competition and higher salaries.

Where will the funding for these new initiatives come from? It is essential that we not only communicate to the university administration that the role of the library has been completely transformed by providing examples of enhanced services that provide added value to the academic community; we must demonstrate the worth of those services. There is no better publicity for the library than the testimony of satisfied users—especially when it reaches the ears of the deans and the provost. Returning to the theme of reorganization, finding ways to redirect positions that previously supported functions we can now abandon or adjust can offer a creative solution that permits us to meet new needs. As we publicize our successes, we also develop a more compelling case to attract donor funding, particularly if we are embarking on a capital campaign. Packaging opportunities to support the library in new ways that convey the dynamism of our people and our services, as well as their vital connections to faculty and students, is another way to attract the resources needed. Inviting potential donors to come and see firsthand how the library has changed, how we have emerged from the gray times, can stimulate new contributions and long-term, productive relationships.

## *SPACE AS CATALYST*

While a new and/or expanded building is, obviously, not required to bring about the changes needed to move the library fully out of the gray times, it certainly has been a major impetus for change at Duke. The Perkins Project, the renovation and expansion of the libraries, comprises multiple phases that will be completed over several years. Such an ongoing project could be seen as a disadvantage (construction noise, disruption, confused users), but in fact it has had a silver lining: the ability to learn as we go, to observe how the new spaces are being used, and to introduce changes or adaptations in subsequent phases. For example, our new building opened in fall 2005 and a year later we relocated the reference desk—not far, but to a place that makes much more sense given the traffic patterns between our two main connected buildings. We have reconfigured the furniture in The Perk, our coffeehouse, in response to students' requests for ample library study tables to replace some of the smaller café tables, which are more suitable for one-on-one consultations. We have redistributed the functions of the public documents and maps department, creating a new service point for GIS and Data Services. The list goes on.

Perhaps most significant of all, we are moving our technical services operations offsite to a newly remodeled location a ten-minute campus bus ride away, more spacious and comfortable than their original intended destination in our renovated building. This relocation is enabling us to implement a limited reorganization, to consolidate technical services for public documents and for special collections, along with gifts processing (formerly within Collection Development) with our main acquisitions, cataloging, and electronic resources/serials units. The space that had been earmarked for technical services onsite will now house the Teaching and Learning Center described earlier. Staff that will move offsite have been fully engaged in planning for their new "home" in everything from furniture selection to ergonomics and workflow analysis, building design to parking and outdoor beautification. The libraries' popularity following the renovation led directly to the decision to emphasize and expand user services onsite. As we proceed through the next phases, we will continue to observe and to listen to students and other library users and adapt both services and spaces to meet existing needs and anticipate new ones. The building is just a shell without a well-designed and effective program inside, but careful design of the building should facilitate the successful implementation of that program.

## IN CONCLUSION: TELL THE STORY OF SUCCESS

No one can really see into the future, digital or otherwise. We do our best to see around the next corner, to predict, based on trends, studies, and observations, what research libraries might be like, could be like, and should be like in the years ahead. One thing is clear: the roles of various units on our campuses are blending and converging when they used to be clearly separate. The recent Ithaka report, *University Publishing in a Digital Age*,[6] suggests that libraries and university presses should form new partnerships; the development and management of digital repositories will call on the expertise of campus information technology staff as well as archivists and digital collections experts within the library. A 2008 article in the *Chronicle of Higher Education* suggested there should be a closer relationship between university IT operations and libraries and that they each have a great deal to contribute to planning for technological changes within the university.[7] All of this suggests that changes we are facing include not just intra-library cooperation of a sort that we have not traditionally seen but much broader university-wide collaboration across units that have had separate orbits, a dynamic that did not really exist in the gray times. Our paths will intersect more and more; our ability to lead libraries and to thrive in the digital future will be dependent on forging close relationships on campus and beyond.

As we know, the traditional image of the library, its people and its services, as well as it may have served in the gray times, has not kept up with the current reality. Dramatic change is evident in every aspect of our operations, collections, spaces, attitudes, and philosophy of service. The pace of this change may seem breathtakingly rapid at times, piling on new responsibilities that require competence with an array of skills that have not been part of our tool kit and prompting library staff to update their knowledge almost constantly. Our leadership will be essential to the creation of an environment in which change is welcomed, as is the chance to play an even larger and more significant role in the intellectual lives of students and faculty. We need only catch our collective breath, confidently seize the opportunities that are coming our way, and set loose the best thinking among our talented staffs. The success story of the research library needs to be told more broadly, more loudly, and in full color, well beyond the walls of our busy buildings.

## NOTES

1. Oldenburg, Ray, *The Great Good Place: Cafés, Coffee Shops, Bookstores, Bars, Hair Salons and other Hangouts at the Heart of a Community* (New York: Marlowe & Co., 1999).

2. *The 2003 Environmental Scan: Pattern Recognition* (Dublin, OH: OCLC Online Computer Library Center, Inc, 2004), 60.

3. Wilder, Stanley, *ARL Bimonthly Report 254* (Washington, DC: Association of Research Libraries, 2007), 3.

4. Neal, James G., "Raised by Wolves: Integrating the New Generation of Feral Professionals into the Academic Library," February 15, 2006 http://www.libraryjournal.com/article/CA6304405.html (accessed June 23, 2008).

5. http://www.arl.org/rtl/escience/eresource.shtml (accessed June 23, 2008).

6. Brown, Laura, Griffiths, Rebecca, Rascoff, Matthew, *University Publishing in a Digital Age* (New York: Ithaka, June 2007).

7. Foster, Andrea, "Strains and Joys Color Merger Between Libraries and Technology Units," *Chronicle of Higher Education*, January 18, 2008.

# Index

*The Academic Library and the Net Gen Student: Making the Connections* (Gibbons) 41, 42
access 3, 15, 22; culture of 5, 17; free public 21; improving 80; long-term 15; open 25; policies on 88; reducing barriers to 61; round the clock 108
access and use policies 18
acquisitions 15, 103
ACRLog 43
Adams, Megan M. 33
affordability 3
*Agenda for Developing E-Science in Libraries*: (ARL) 114
alert services 61
Aluka 48
alumni 115
Amazon.com 7
American Council of Learned Societies 18
American Historical Association 24
Andrew Mellon Foundation 73, 112
archives 15, 49, 50, 81, 95, 99, 100; digital scientific data 97
archivists 40
Arms, Professor William: Cornell University 23
articles: online delivery 108
arXiv: Cornell University 22
assessment: culture of 5-7
Association of American Publishers (AAP) 75
Association of College and Reference Libraries (ACRL): *Top Ten Assumptions for the Future of Libraries and Librarians* 39-40
Association of College and Research Libraries (ACRL): *Libraries and the Post-Job Organization* 31

Association of Research Libraries (ARL) 22, 83; 2006 survey 20; *Agenda for Developing E-Science in Libraries* 114; SPEC Kit on Metadata 19, 20
astronomy 22
Australia 80; libraries 33
authority 112
authors 71, 74; rights 40, 88; tools for 100

bandwidth 72; United States Congress 72
Barrett, Laura 11
Beile, Penny. M 33
Bengtson, Betty: University of Washington Libraries 5
bibliographer 32, 101
*Bibliotheque Nationale* 71
bioscientists 6
Blackboard 68, 115
The Blake Archive: University of Virginia Library 24
blogs 3, 38, 39, 42, 69
book: culture of 5
BookExpo America (2006) 70-71
books: rare 41
bookshelves: virtual 70
Braille 11-12
Bridges, William 39, 43; *JobShift* 31; "The End of the Job" *Fortune* 31
Brown University Library: Center for Digital Initiatives 19, 25
budget 5; flexible 110; materials 115

C++ 33
California Digital Library 26; eScholarship Publishing Program 24
capacity: problem with 72
Carnegie Mellon University: copyright 69; "Million Book Project" 69

cataloging 15, 103; local 102; systems 97
catalogs: online 112
CDRom networks 35
Center for Digital Initiatives: Brown University Library 19
Centre for Learning and Performance Technologies: Google 69
CGI scripts 33
change: culture of 5; fear of 113; librarians and 48; opportunities for 62; resistance to 57
chat 39, 99, 108
Choi, Youngok 33
Choudhury, G. Sayeed: Johns Hopkins University 18, 25
*Chronicle of Higher Education* 117
circulation 10
citations: dissertations 15
classification: history of 92
coffeehouse 107
collaboration 4-5, 101; barriers to 5; successful 5
collaborative research 109
collections 100, 101-103; development 102; digital 108, 111; general 102; hidden 15; local 41; management 101; on-line 106; print 108; selection 41; shared print 41; special 2, 15, 52, 95, 106; unique 41
*College and Research Libraries News* 34
*College and Research Libraries News* advertisements: Lynch and Smith 33
Columbia University Library 24
Columbia University Press 24
Committee on Institutional Cooperation (CIC) 23
community: culture of 5
conference: Web casts 39
consulting services 40
content 92
copying 100
copyright 15, 16, 22, 25; 2006 BookExpo Convention debate 71; awareness and management 21; Carnegie Mellon University 69; constraints 9; Fair Use

clause 77; flexible policies 83; Google Book Search Project 68; job role of librarian 40; management 85; NIH policy-friendly 86; OCA 76; officers 86; owners 17; transfer agreements 83
Cornell University: Arms, Professor William 23; arXiv 22
Cornell University Library: Digital Consulting & Production Services (DCAPS) 19, 25; Google Book Search Project 69
cost 7
Council on Library and Information Resources 73
course management software 68
credibility 93
Croenis, Karen. S 33
cultural heritage 94, 95, 96
curation: long-term 9; university business records 95
curriculum: online 41
cyberinfrastructure 18
*cyberscholarship* 23
cyberscholarship 25

data management 101
databases 110; development 37
Datanet grant program 18
datasets 52
Dempsey, Lorcan 4
desktop delivery 6
detail: culture of 5
developing countries 9
DIALOG 31, 35
digital age: and faculty 15-17
digital archives: preservation 73
digital authorship 42
digital collections 108
digital content 102
digital delivery: just-in-time 102
digital information: trends in 93
digital infrastructure 91
digital librarians 33, 36
digital libraries 3, 4, 36
digital preservation 58

## Index

digital publishing 98
digital repositories 20-23
digital resources: librarians expertise in management of 16
digital tools 57; savings 64
digitization 15, 16, 101, 102; future applications of 77; global mass stores 93; impact of 76; journals 73; mass 23, 69; services 18-20, 99; skills 37, *see also* Large-Scale Digitization Initiatives (LSDI), Google Book Search Project
dissemination: research 80
dissertations: citations 15
Dolan, Donna R. 32, 33
Duderstadt, James: University of Michigan 2
Duke University: Data Services 111; Perkins Project 116; Teaching and Learning Center 109
Duke University Library 108

e-books 41
e-journal 6
e-journal back files 110
e-mail 39
e-mail reference service 108
e-reserves 108, 115
e-resources 106
e-scholarship 22
e-Scholarship Publishing Program: University of California 24
e-science 22-23, 25
Ebrary 70
economics 58-63; changing research patterns in 60-62
economists: attitudes to electronic resources 60; attitudes to print 60; belief in gateway role 59; dependence on library **59**; and the internet 62; perception of library 59-60
editor contracts 25
Elecronic Publishing Initiative @ Columbia (EPIC) 26
electronic access 6
electronic full-text 10

Electronic Reference Librarian 35
electronic resource management systems 103
Electronic Resources 36; attitudes of economists 60
Electronic Services Librarian 35, 36
Elsevier: Springer-Verlag 75
embargo period: PubMed Central (PMC) 84
environmental scanning 6
eScholarship Publishing Program: California Digital Library 24
European Union 80

faculty 92; attitudes towards libraries 48-55; and digital age 15-17; and library 14; needs and priorities 6; partnering 26; and technology 70; view of role of librarian 48; views of importance of librarians **49**; views on irrelevance of library **50**
Fair Use clause: copyright 77
Farkas, Meredith: *Information Wants to be Free* 42, 43
Fert, Albert 67
findability 22
*First Monday*: Morrison, Heather 38
Fisher, William 33
formats 18
France: critic of Google Book Search Project 71
Friedman, Thomas: *The World is Flat* 68
funding 9, 114

Genbank 22, 85
Genome-Wide Association Studies data repository 22
Gibbons, Susan: *The Academic Library and the Net Gen Student: Making the Connections* 41, 42, 44
GIS 111, 116
global research library 7-10
Global Research Library 2020 (GRL2020) 8; impediments 9-10
global research library: core values 8-9; infrastructure 9
globalization 30

Google 23, 34, 36, 39; Centre for Learning and Performance Technologies 69; as a competitor 63, 65; as a discovery tool 51; impact of 76; and libraries 101
Google Book Search Project 68; copyright 68; Cornell University library 69; criticism from France 71; goals 73; problems with 73-75; University of Michigan 68
Google Print 34
Google Publishing Partners 73
Google Scholar 69
Gopher 35
grad students 96
*The Great Good Place* 107
Greenspan, Alan 77
group work 110
Gruenberg, Peter 67

*Harvard Gazette* 21
Harvard University: Faculty of Arts and Sciences 20; institutional repository (IR) 20
Henderson, Pat 33
Hey, Tony 8
Highwire Press: Stanford University Library 24
hosting: journals 16
HTML literacy 33
humanities 64, 97; dependence on libraries 53; online research 60; and print journals 56; view of librarians 49
Huskies 2

Illiad 10
ILSare 98
information: availability of 8
information lifecycle management 40
information literacy 4
*Information Literacy Competency Standards* 37
information literacy instruction 99
information mediation and interpretation 41-42
information technology 6

Information Technology Librarian 35
*Information Wants to be Free*: (Farkas) 42
infrastructure: global research library 9
instant messaging (IM) 39, 99, 108
Institute for Museum and Library Services: 21st Century Librarian grants 40, 42
institutional repository (IR) 38; Harvard University 20; strategy 21
intellectual community: creating 107-108
intellectual property 9, 40
Inter-University Consortium for Political and Social Research 22
interdisciplinarity 109-111
interface 92
interlibrary loan 10, 15, 41, 73, 102, 110
International Organization for Economic Cooperation and Development 80
Internet 35, 44; and economists 62; infrastructure 72; opportunities 80; and Reference Librarians 31
Internet Archive 76
Internet Explorer 34
interoperability 18
inventory control 103
iPod 34, 67
irrational exuberance 77
Italian National Research Council: Institute of Information Science and Technologies (CNR-ITSI) 10
Ithaka 63; research 47-48; university publishing 18; *University Publishing in a Digital Age* 117

*Janus in Cyberspace: Archives on the Threshold of the Digital Era*: Pearce-Moses, Richard 44
job advertisements 33; technology 38
job announcements: librarians 34-38
job titles: electronically enhanced 35; librarians 34
Johns Hopkins University: Choudhury, G. Sayeed 18; Digital Research and Curation Center 18; Project Muse 24; Virtual Observatory (VO) 18
journals 23; article gestation 60;

cancellation of subscriptions 55; copyright policies of 82; cost of electronic 115; digitization 73; electronic version 55; hosting 16; humanities and print version 56; manuscripts 15; open access 16; price 25; profitability 74; subscriptions 80; support for cancellation of printed version **56**; support for electronic version **56**; support for maintaining hard copy collection **57**; transition away from print 55-58

JSTOR 47, 58, 73; resistance to from historians 58

JULIET database 82

junior faculty 96

just-in-time: digital delivery 102

Kahle, Brewster 76

Kelly, Kevin: *Out of Control* 71; *Wired* 71

Kelly, Kevin *Out of Control* 71

Kennan, Mary Anne 33

keywords: inaccuracy of 74

knowledge 8

LANs 35

Large-Scale Digitization Initiatives (LSDI) 72

Lassie 105

learning: technology enhanced 74

Leeder, Kim 93

legal counsel 83; compliance role 85-87

lending 100

Lessing, Doris 71

LibQUAL 6

librarians 74, 94; 2006 survey 52; attitude and behaviors 47-48; author rights 88; and change 48; changing roles 112; digital 33; digital job titles 36; Electronic Service 36; electronically enhanced job titles 35; evolution of positions 40; expertise in managing digital resources 16; "feral" 113; four new core responsibilities 40-43; function rating **53**; and humanities faculty 49; job announcements 34-38; job titles 34-38; National Institute of Health (NIH) 87-89; new renaissance 42; new roles and responsibilities 30; next generation 113; and open access 69; opportunities for 88-89; overcoming resistance 114; perceived key roles 52; position descriptions 32; reference 31, 32, 36; resistance to change 57; role of middle managers 113; role of 100-101; and scientists 49; skills 97-99; subject 32, 34-37, 40, 102; systems 32, 33, 37; training 115; United Kingdom 34; view of role by faculty 48; views on importance of role by faculty **49**; wandering job titles 38; workflow 43

libraries: 24 hour service 107, 107-108, 115; adding value 63; allocating resources 94; Australia 33; authority of 112; building 93; buildings 99, 106, 109; catalog 54; changing roles of 50-53; and competition 63; complex role of 106; considering disciplinary differences 64; core mission and values 91; deconstructing and redefining 93-94; delivering resources 99-103; dependence of economists **59**; dependence on 53-55; developing niche services 96; donors 115; engaging with faculty 63-64; and faculty 14; faculty attitudes toward 48-55; food and drink policies 107; future of 42; as a gateway 50; as a gateway - views on **52**; global research 7-10; goals 91; and Google 101; and humanities 53; importance of participation 17-18; importance of roles by discipline **51**; large 54; marketing 111, 115; and Microsoft 101; mission of 2, 9; missions 94-96; as organizing systems 92; partnership with campus IT 95, 117; perceptions of economists 59-60; popularity 116; as purchaser 50; recommendations for 63-65; reorganizing; retraining and rethinking 111; research 53-54; responsive and

flexible 108-109; role in digital future 91; role of 115; satellites 110; and scientists 53; seating options 107; security 107, 115; services and skills 97-99; shape and form of emerging 3; and social scientists 53; strategies 7; traditional image of 117; understanding changing faculty needs 63-64; users 96-97; as a verb 93; view of by scientists 50; views on its irrelevance by faculty **50**
Library 2.0: incorporating 111
*Library Hi Tech* 33
Library Web Manager 36
licensing 38
literature review 32-34
long-term curation 9, 17
Lynch, Beverly P.: *College and Research Libraries News* advertisements 33

McGraw-Hill 70
magnetoresistance 67
maps 116
mash-ups 3
Mellon Foundation 73, 112
memory: culture of 5
metadata 16, 18, 22, 25, 103; contributing 111; developing 95; librarians as advisers 98
metadata services 18-20
Microsoft 8, 76; and libraries 101; mass digitization project 69
Miller, Rush: *Journal of Academic Librarianship* 39
missions: library 2, 9
MIT 37, 86
MLS: future of 112
monographs 23, 49
Morrison, Heather: *First Monday* 38
Mosaic 35
multidisciplinary scholarship 7
MySpace 91

National Bureau of Economic Research (NBER) 60

National Institutes of Health (NIH): awareness 86; contract 81; grant 81; intramural program 81; librarians 87-89; open access 40, 75; Public Access Policy 81-89; PubMed Central (PMC) 22, 79, 82-89; researchers 81
National Library of Medicine *See* National Institutes of Health (NIH)
National Science Foundation (NSF) 11, 18
Netscape 34
network (global) level: moving to 10
networked environment 2
*New York Times Magazine* 71
NITLE 48
Nobel Prize: Literature 71; Physics 67
Noory, George 77

OCLC 75; WorldCat Local 10
Odyssey 47
Office of Digital Scholarly Publishing (ODSP): Penn State 24
Office of Sponsored Research 83
online: curriculum 41; systems development 15
online courses 74
online research 60
online-information: remote use of 6
OPAC 97, 98
open access 9, 79-81; blocking 75; journal 16; and librarians 69; movement 38; National Institutes for Health 40, 75
Open Content Alliance (OCA) 76
Open Journal Systems (OJS) 25, 26
Orbis Cascade Alliance 10
ordering systems: vendor 103
organization 15
*Out of Control*: (Kelly) 71

Palm Pilot 34
Partnership for Research Integrity in Science and Medicine (PRISM) 75
*Pattern Recognition* 107
Pearce-Moses, Richard: *Janus in Cyberspace: Archives on the Threshold of the Digital Era* 44

Pearce-Moses, Richard *Janus in Cyberspace: Archives on the Threshold of the Digital Era* 44
Penn State: Office of Digital Scholarly Publishing (ODSP) 24
*Penn State Romance Studies* 24
Perkins Project: Duke University 116
philosophy 56
Pinfield, Stephen 34, 43
place: meaning of 42; undergraduates 6
podcasts 99
popularity: measurements 61
Portico 48
postjob library redux 39-43
Power Point 69
preservation 15, 17, 22, 25, 94, 98; digital archives 73; risks in digital system 58
Princeton University 76
print: attitudes of economists 60; transition away from 55-58
print transition: risks in 58
Project Muse: Johns Hopkins University 24
protocol standards 9
Prouest 73
*Provocative Statements*: Taiga Forum (2006) 40
PubChem 85
public access: goals and benefits 87; the issues 79-81
public access policy: National Institutes of Health (NIH) 81-89
public funding 79; improving accountability 81
public investments: social returns 80
public value 8
publication cycle 61
publishers 74; textbook cost 70
publishing 18, 23-25, 97; alternative outlets 40; electronic 9; instant 61; scholarly 4
PubMed 85
PubMed Central (PMC) 22, 79, 82-89; approval 84; citation 84-85; depositing a manuscript in 84, 88; embargo period 84; impact on researchers 85

PubMed Central (PMC) *See also* National Institutes for Health (NIH)
Purdue 37

Quechua 11-12

rapid document delivery 41
Rasmussen, Edie 33
*Readers Guide to Periodical Literature* 31
reference 99
reference desk 39
Reference Librarian: and the internet 31
Reference Librarian for Networked Resources 35
Reference/Database Access Librarian 35
RePEc 63
repositories 9, 40, 81, 100; decentralizing 23; digital 115; disciplinary 22, *see also* institutional repository (IR)
research 79; accelerating pace of 80; changing patterns in economics 60-62; collaborative 109; dissemination 80; new 60; policies for sharing 80-81; starting points for 51, 54
research data 3
research and development culture 42
research libraries *see* libraries
Research Papers in Economics (RePEc) 61
researchers 74; clinical 96; impact of PubMed Central (PMC) 85; roles complying with NIH access policy 82-85
review process 61
reward systems 5
rights: retaining 82
rights management 88
risks: in print transition 58
Rosetti Archive 24
RSS feeders 69

scholarly communication 4, 115; support 98
Scholarly Publishing Office: University of Michigan 24
Scholar's Copyright Addendum Engine (SCAE) 83
scholarship: long-term survival of 17

Schumacher, John 32, 33
Science Commons 83, 86
scientists 64; and libraries 53; view on library 50; views on librarians 49
search engines 2
search linking tools 101
seating options: libraries 107
SecondLife 91
security: libraries 107, 115
selection 9, 15
self-reliance 6
sharing 9; information and research 80
SHERPA/ROMEO database 82
Shieber, Stuart 21
Shulenburger, David 18
Smith, Kimberley Robles: *College and Research Libraries News* advertisements 33
social networking 42
Social Science Research Network (SSRN) 61
social scientists: and libraries 53; online research 60
Society of American Archivists 44
SPARC 34, 83, 86
SPARC Author addendum 83
SPEC Kit on Metadata: Association of Research Libraries (ARL) 19, 20
special collections *see* collections
stacks: offsite facilities 110
Stanford University Library: Highwire Press 24
Stoffle, Carla 93
structures 15, 18
students 92; and desire for technology 70
surveys 6
sustainability 9
Suzzallo Library 2
Suzzallo, President Henry: University of Washington (UW) 1, 12

Tactile Graphics Project 11
Taiga Forum (2006): *Provocative Statements* 40
technology 30; challenges and opportunities of 31-32; culture of 5; enhanced learning 74; impact on scholarly communication 37; job advertisements 38; and students 70
telecommunications 9
textbooks: cost of 69
*The World is Flat*: (Friedman) 68
*Top Ten Assumptions for the Future of Libraries and Librarians*: Association of College and Reference Libraries (ACRL) 39-40
Torrero, Alfredo 11-12
trust 112
trustees 92
Tutor.com 108
Twain, Mark 24

undergraduates 96; place 6
United Kingdom 80; librarians 34
United States of America 80
United States Congress: bandwidth 72
university: digital academic assets 94, 95
university administrators 81; compliance role 85-7
University of California: e-Scholarship Publishing Program 24
University of California Press 26
University of Michigan 20; Duderstadt, James 2; Google Book Search Project 68; Scholarly Publishing Office 24
University of Nebraska: The Walt Whitman Archive 24
university publishing: Ithaka 18
*University Publishing in a Digital Age*: (Ithaka) 117
University of Virginia Library 24
University of Washington Libraries 3, 8; Bengtson, Betty 5
University of Washington (UW): Suzzallo, President Henry 1
Updike, John 71
usability testing 6
user community 92
users 42; focus on 5; libraries 96-97; satisfying 115

Valley of the Shadow: University of Virginia 24
value-added services 55
Velaro 108
virtual assistance 39
virtual environment 54
virtual library 6
Virtual Observatory (VO): John Hopkins University 18
*Vision 2010*: University of Washington Libraries 3
vocabularies 15

The Walt Whitman Archive: University of Nebraska 24
Web 2.0 capabilities 9, 41
Web casts: conference 39
Web Development Librarian 36
*Web of Science* 7

Web Services Librarian 36
web sites: branding and nesting 100; design 19
White, Gary W. 33
Wikipedia 111; debate 114
wikis 38, 42
Wilder, Stanley 112
Willard, Patricia 33
Wilson, Betsy 93
Wilson, Concepcion S. 33
working papers 60
working papers network 61
World Wide Web 44; publications 61; searches 61
WorldCat Local: OCLC 10
WorldCat.org 10

Yahoo 76
YouTube 34